Soul Searchers

Gail Webb

This is a work of true account; some names have been
changed some are original

This book highlights just some of the true cases of
hauntings and attachments I have worked on as well as
inclusion of my own personal journey.

ISBN: 1981180885
ISBN-13: 978-1981180882

DEDICATION

This book is dedicated to all those who have been brave and have allowed me to publish the trauma and destructive energy they have experienced in their lives and of the agonizing wait not knowing of the whereabout of their loved one.

These people's true accounts are what has compelled me to write this book. Hauntings and spirit attachments do happen and is more common than some would like to think.

To Matthew Manning, a fellow author whose work I have admired for many years who has written a review. http://matthewmanning.net

To my friend Yancy and his daughters Katrina and Laura for their patience of reading the chapters as proof readers and to my dear friend Tracy for always being there.

To my family Kelly and Kevin, Steve and Abbey and my grandchildren Elise and Connor who I love with all my heart. Throughout their lives they have witnessed many strange happenings that have happened around me that may have at times concerned them.

Prologue

As a natural medium, growing up was not easy for me, especially during puberty. A time when my psychic abilities were rife. Friendships and relationships, I felt were thwarted once they knew I had the ability to speak with the dead.

It was in the early seventies, a time when spiritual phenomena weren't popular or easily spoken about. The film the Exorcist was showing at a local cinema and I clearly remember priests standing on the steps handing out leaflets about the devil and his work, discouraging people from seeing the film.

I had formed a friendship with a girl of my own age and who had also experienced very similar phenomena to me. She had come from a family whose father was a practising medium who had since died. She lived with her mother, a non-believer who had tried everything to discourage her daughter from going in the same footsteps as he.

It had been difficult at times for me to block out the many spirit connections who wanted to speak with me. Over time I learnt how to control the constant chatter I could hear inside my head. There were so many.

I did not ask for this inheritance nor did I go to any schools of learning. Naturally, as friends we had a lot in common and had felt comfortable in each other's company.

One evening whilst she was visiting my home, my father was upstairs asleep in bed. He had always been a light sleeper. we were sitting in the lounge, just talking about everyday things teenagers talked about. She was sat at one end of the corner sofa and myself at the other end. Whilst we were talking, we had noticed the electric fire had turned on. The electric bulb had warmed up sending the little fan around in circles giving an illusion of a flame. The plug had laid on the floor and was not connected to the socket.

A mumbling sound of unknown origin could be heard and it seemed to be getting louder. We had simultaneously looked around the room to find the source and at first, had thought it to have been the aquarium but then knew differently. She was alarmed and had jumped up with a frightened expression on her face. I had jumped too as I had felt uneasy. She had backed away from me heading for the lounge door. She was struggling to turn the door handle, screaming at me *"I saw your face changed, into a man's, a black man. Get away from me. I want to get out"*. The sound had intensified blocking out her words until it became impossible to hear her.

I thought it was strange my father hadn't come downstairs demanding us to be quiet. I too had tried the door handle and although it moved down easily it did not release. The door was firmly shut. It was as if an invisible force was holding on to it. It was at this point that she accepted I too experienced the same predicament as her. She was panicking and had run over to the Velux window. The handle had moved fully but it did not dislodge the catch.

A pungent smell of something rotting permeated the whole room making it feel very uncomfortable. Neither of us knew what was happening, having never experienced anything of this nature before. We were trapped together in the room with no escape. She looked over at me in disbelief. I knew as a sensitive that she had felt the same as me, there was something dark yet to come.

From the corner of the room, a dark mass was beginning to materialise into a thick black fog like substance. Within seconds three images had appeared. They were monks. All had worn brown habits. The one in the centre had held an opened book in his hands. The other two had held their heads bowed and seemed to be focused on the book. The disorientating mumbling sound had changed. I could clearly hear it was the monks chanting. The hairs on the back of my neck had stood up.

In my peripheral view, I could see my friend was clearly shaken. She was shouting out the Lord's Prayer. This seemingly having no effect what so ever. The monks were floating towards me hovering a few inches from the ground. The bottom of their habits didn't touch the floor. Soon, I was eye to eye with the one in the middle. His face was like a rotting corpse. The skull was partially revealed with bits of exposed decomposing flesh. I was extremely frightened. I had never felt a darkness or threat like it. My friend was frantically rattling the door trying to escape.

The monks focused their attention towards me, ignoring my friend. His evil eyes bore deep into my own. He locked me in his glare for what seemed like an eternity but in reality, was probably only seconds. I knew he was trying to implant his thoughts into mine trying to take over my mind. The chanting was having a hypnotic effect upon me. Suddenly, a surge of energy originating from my right arm, like an electric shock, ran through my entire body. This was enough to break my connection with the monk.

With my back pressed hard against the door, I felt an immense pressure around my neck. My cross and chain I wore had started to float upwards. The chain now stretched out. My focus was drawn to the crucifix as I watched it slowly turn into an upright position revealing its engraving. It was like something out of a horror movie. I called out for my guide to help me. I was so frightened.

I remember so vividly, feeling as if I had grown in stature and height, I was looking down upon them. I felt so strong inside like a steel door. I shouted out, *'I am not afraid of you. You must be gone and leave this plane, you are not wanted here. You must find solace and peace elsewhere.'* These words were coming from my mouth, but they were not of my tongue, a deep tone of a man's voice came out from my voice box.

Suddenly my chain had dropped and was no longer suspended in mid-air. The chanting had ceased. There was a deafening quietness to the room. The lounge door had made a clicking noise and it had opened with ease. We both ran out of the house and into the street. Frightened and bewildered by the encounter. We walked towards the town centre both talking at once with neither of us making any sense of what just happened.

However, our torment was not yet over!

We sat down on the bench that was placed in the newly refurbished shopping centre. We were so absorbed in our own experience that we didn't notice anything much of our surroundings. We knew the town really well both having grown up in the area.

During our conversation, I'd felt my right arm tingling, similar to pins and needles but ten times worse. The feeling I previously experienced of being taller and stronger came flooding back into my limbs. It was just as I was describing these sensations to my friend when I heard a man's voice talk deep inside my head. It said *"turn your back towards hers, back to back. You will not be harmed"* On telling my friend she yelled, "Oh no not again".

We heard a lot of excited male voices that were getting closer to us. They had come into full view and were approaching us. There were five of them in total. All of them were acting in an intoxicated manner and was obviously out for a bit of fun. They were much older than ourselves possibly in their mid-thirties.

We had both felt petrified. My friend had wanted to run, but I had grabbed her arm for her to remain still. I reminded her what the voice had said. Keep your back pressed tightly against mine and you will be ok. I didn't know who was the most scared. I could feel my adrenaline pump through my body with a rush. I was in a fight or flight response and knew I had to stand my ground.

I was face to face with them. The bulkier one of the five men had stepped forward away from the rest of the group. He acted in a bravado mannerism and had held a bottle of beer in his hand. He wore a ridiculous grin on his face as he came up to me at close range looking me up and down.

I could see he was displaying nervous tension and was transferring his weight from one foot to the other, awaiting his strike. The other four men in the group held back laughing and taking delight in my obvious discomfort. I could feel the tension in my friends back as she had pushed herself closer into me. I asked *'what do you want'*, he replied *'you'* The others began to laugh finding it highly amusing. I mentally called my guides in to help me, for the second time this evening. I remember focusing my energy and had become somewhat disengaged from the situation emotionally.

I had smiled at him in the hope of unnerving him. He had read the signal wrong and had moved closer towards me, reaching out his arm to grab me around my waist. My right arm had thrust out gathering up his T-shirt, into my fist. His body had lifted easily without strain.

There was no effort in lifting his heavy frame. I had thrown him, like a paper dart, where he proceeded to travel through the glass panel of a local shoe shop, activating the alarm. The alarm had brought me back into a consciousness state of mind I didn't know I had slipped from. My friend kept saying *"oh my God are you ok? That was awesome"!*

His friends had run off.
We both walked quickly away from the scene.

The following day I was so affected by the incident and was still experiencing this strange tingling in my arm. I was frightened I had become possessed.

We decided to seek the advice and help of a local Vicar, not knowing where else to turn. We visited his home later that day. He had welcomed us both into his home and had wanted us to explain the previous evening's events to him in detail.

Throughout our excited statement, he would nod and interject asking us about the smallest of details. We had told him everything even the assault in the precinct.

He seemed to be particularly interested in the sensation I had felt in my arm and of the feeling of being tall and strong. After hearing my side of events, he turned around had questioned my friend of her account. She had described how early in the evening my facial features had changed into a black mans and of the super strength I seemed to be demonstrating.

After some moments he spoke *"I understand what has happened"* He stood up and reached up to a bookcase behind him and took down the Holy Bible together with a small box from the shelf. He opened the box and extracted a small bottle with a silk sash.

He kissed the sash before placing it around his neck. Neither of us had said anything. My mind was racing with what he may do next. He opened the bottle and had asked me to raise my right arm and roll up my sleeve. I hadn't told him what arm I'd received the tingling sensation. How did he know it was my right one? However, I did feel I could trust him so I did as he asked. He began to sprinkle holy water over it. He asked me to visualise my arm as a snake, shedding its skin. I had felt a slight stinging sensation but that was all. He brushed invisible crumbs away from around my body. After I asked him what he was doing. He replied, *"I'm cleansing and freeing you of any residual negative energy"*.

I questioned him how he knew it was my right arm and what was the meaning of our experience? He explained, *"we were both sensitives which give us the ability to sense subtle spirit energies"*. He went on to say that *"You have been chosen to work in a particular spiritual field. To understand the energy of the Dark side"*. He advised me to take note of how to cleanse the aura as I would need to become familiar with this as I go forward with my path of learning spiritual matters.

He told me, *"To become a good teacher, one has to be first a student. This experience was gifted to you, for you to learn how it feels to be overcome by the dark side, at first hand. Your guide and protector came forth. Do not have fear in your heart as you will have him stand by your side when you encounter dark energies"*.

He continued to say as time goes on, he will reveal more of himself, as trust grows and deepens, for without complete trust, we have no faith.

He told me in confidence that he too receives voice messages, I asked him, from God? He smiled. I questioned him further *"are you like us, can you hear and see spirit"*? He gave no comment.

Summary:
Many years have passed since my first experience of being attacked by a dark entity. This experience saw my first initiation of having Zulu my protective guide work beside me.

There are a number of different classes of demons. Shapeshifters are one of the darkest to encounter. They have the ability reflect an image such as a monk or a young defensive child in order to deflect from who they really are, lowering our defences of evil intent. They are non-human entities whose goal is domination and procession of the soul.

Lower level entities are not as advanced or feared. The Vicar was correct, my Zulu guide has shown himself to me many times and to others, who have witnessed seeing him when accompanying me on a case, where dark energies have been present. He appears as around 7ft tall, with a toned blue-black skin. He has a powerful physique and personality. He stands with a spear and an oval shaped animal skinned shield.

He had allowed a photo to be taken of himself during one of my Physical Mediumship workshops. I had asked him to pop his arm out of the spirit cabinet, he did not disappoint me.

CONTENTS

ACKNOWLEDGMENTS

Thankyou to Matthew Manning for his review as below

"Over the decades I've been fortunate to have known some of the greatest mediums of all time - stars of the psychic world such as Doris Stokes, Gordon Higginson, Douglas Johnson and Doris Collins. They were sought after and revered because of the quality of evidence they gave in their readings and demonstrations, always giving the names of loved ones, personal information known only to a small number of close family members and often addresses. Mediums of that caliber are rare and, sadly, they have all long since passed away.

Thankfully, a very small handful of people now follow in their footsteps - and without any doubt Gail Webb is one of them.

Her gifts as a medium are extraordinary and, in my opinion, she joins the pantheon of those great mediums. Her readings are simply amazing. Without 'fishing' for information she rapidly relays names, dates and information about departed loved ones. You can almost believe they are alive and with you in the room. I have met many people who have had the privilege of a reading with her and all of them have been similarly speechless afterwards.

For those who wonder how she does it, this book is a wonderful introduction. It's full of gripping accounts of hauntings and spiritual disturbances that, with her mediumship, Gail has been able to resolve and heal. I found it so gripping that I read it in one sitting"!

Matthew Manning

Chapter 1

The Night Visitor

From his first word, I had already started tuning into the vibration of the male voice, *'For God's sake, you must help us!'* This wasn't the first time I received a call of this nature, and it won't be the last. Before he uttered another word, I could already feel the darkness, and I knew the threat was real. *'My wife is encountering horrific nightly visits.'* I quickly stopped him before he could tell me anymore. I never want the full details of what is happening, that job is for my guides. They will give me an untainted, transparent and accurate view of the situation. I knew they urgently needed help, so we arranged an immediate appointment.

After the phone call, sitting quietly, I opened my mind to telepathic communication with my guides. A form of remote viewing took place where images were projected within my mind. These fragments of information were shown to me like the first pieces of a puzzle, yet to be understood and placed, but still creating their own little picture of important key issues associated with the case. My guides again confirmed this was an urgent matter.

The couple was David and Brenda. I met up with them on a January afternoon. The weather was very bleak with a heaviness in the air. I'd felt a little apprehensive driving through the electric gates onto their elegant tree-lined driveway that swept up to the panelled front door. An overwhelming sensation of being watched came over me It took David several years to put together the beautiful five bedroomed property, of which had seen several renovations, joining together the outbuilding with the old cottage, making it one large dwelling. Around two years ago, David invited Brenda to live with him. As I drove closer I could see they were stood in the doorway waiting to greet me.

Both gave me a warm welcome and were keen to invite me inside, out of the cold. They ushered me through to their lovely warm kitchen where I could smell the fresh coffee that warmed on a percolator. David informed me he bought the former run-down cottage and farmhouse, along with several acres of land as a project, devoting his time and energy to making it the home it is today.

After some light conversation, Brenda revealed she had been experiencing 'visits' on and off, not long after she had moved in. Her latest encounter was only recent. Neither of them had ever experienced anything of this nature before. During our conversation, in my peripheral view, I'd caught sight of a swirling black mass of energy building up near the base of the staircase. This mass, best described as thick cigarette smoke in form, was also seen by the couple. The look of fear in their eyes was clear to see. Upon turning, giving it my full concentration, the black mass had started to dissipate.

Brenda said, *'You're the first person we've asked for help.'* I asked why she had been reluctant to contact anyone before now? Shaking her head nervously, she replied: *'I was frightened and embarrassed to do so.'* Sadly, with my lifetime of experience, this is so often the case.

They both showed me around their home, which was lovingly maintained. It was filled with many artefacts from the different countries they had visited. A beautiful home but one they were seriously considering placing on the market. As we entered each new room, I used my clairsentience, using my body as an antenna, to feel for any residual energy. I pick up on the different density giving me a feel for the amount of spiritual activity taking place in each room.

It was whilst walking along the top landing that I heard a strange humming sound, like that of a small motor. I asked the others what the noise was. David could hear it too. It was coming from behind the closed door of the study. From his expression, he had no idea what it could be.

The sound just outside of the room was very intense. As David opened the door we were met with the distinctive aroma of ectoplasm; that of earthy rotten flesh. Looking in, there were hundreds of bluebottle flies buzzing around the room in a frenzy. They were everywhere completely covering the window; all twitching and struggling, trying to find release. There was an icy chill in the room that had escaped without even stepping inside. With a look of confusion, David commented in disbelief, *'I was only working in the study this morning.'* He had not seen a single fly before this infestation; as you would expect with the cold January conditions. He ran across the room to open the window before going downstairs to get some fly spray, leaving Brenda and myself holding the door slightly ajar.

A few minutes later, David returned with the fly spray. The sound from within was very intense; like a huge generator. We were amazed to see all the flies, one by one, had begun to fall to the ground. Not one tried to escape through the open window. As the bodies fell, the carpet pattern began to fade until it was completely covered by the carcasses of the flies with the room slowly falling silent. David looked down at the can in his hand, stunned, remarking *'I haven't yet used the spray.'* All the flies had seemingly died at the same time. There were so many flies, David used a shovel and several large bin bags to clean up the mass. David scooped several bluebottles into sealed containers to send them off to a pest control centre for analysis.

Brenda and I continued to walk around the house when we came to the Master bedroom. As I stepped through the door, the atmosphere hit me like a ton of bricks. The air was oppressive and heavy. The plaster, behind the door, had been cracked and damaged. My fingers tracing around the damaged wall, I could feel the residual energy was one of anger. Energies can impress themselves into the fabric of our surroundings. As a Medium, I'm able to feel the intensity and download the story of how the impression came to be. Therefore, I ask not to be told the full facts of the incidents a client is experiencing. I don't want to influence the story of which I'm being told. I like to read the house with a clear mind and with no preconceptions to cloud my judgement.

I'd sensed a very strong pull of energy as I gravitated into the room; like metal being dragged towards a magnet. The sensations, that race through my body, are difficult to describe as my receptors resonate with varied vibrations. Walking to the right side of the bed, I'd found myself rooted in place, touching the top of the headboard. This was it. This was the area where I could feel the strongest vibration that I recognized to be a vortex. Brenda had remained quiet as I inspected the room at this stage. With her head down, shoulders hunched and in a very quiet voice she said, *That's my side of the bed...*'

Whilst I stood there, I concentrated on my connection with my guides and the information they were downloading to me. They began to flood my mind with messages and strong impressions. These messages are best described as 3D images. Each image comes with its own set of emotions. My first impression was one of aggression and violence, with a sense of stubbornness. It was a male and he was working alone. He was dominant and wasn't going to go quietly. His total focus and interest were on Brenda. I could see an image reel out within my mind of her hunched up sitting against the headboard. Her emotions were one of panic as she was filled with fear and dread. The impressions that followed were severely disturbing. I understood why she had been reluctant to speak out about her experiences. The entity was an incubus. He was sexually attracted to her and had made his intentions very clear. Brenda was being sexually assaulted by this spirit predator.

David had gone downstairs, leaving Brenda and me alone. It gave me an opportunity to talk with her. We sat down at the end of the bed where I'd asked her straight, *'What's happening?'* I wanted her to reveal to me what she was experiencing. I needed to validate the information that I had received from my guides.

Brenda, with downcast eyes and in her own words, said, *'It wasn't long after moving into the property that I began experiencing lucid dreams of a sexual nature. The attacks begin with experiencing a tingling sensation around my feet that slowly continue up my legs. On some occasions, I've even felt something licking my arm.'* as she shuttered in disgust. *'I could never see anything, but I felt a heavy pressure on my chest. I was being held down. It's at this stage, I experience a form of sleep paralysis, where only my eyes can move. I can hear, and I am aware of the noise within the room, but I lose control over all my limbs.'*

As we sat in the bedroom where the attacks occurred, I needed to stay vigilant. I didn't want to stop Brenda in mid-flow, as I'd felt she'd kept her feelings bottled for so long. Saying this, although I was being empathic and talking to her as one woman to another, I was not forgetting that I was there as a Medium. I was very much attuned to my surroundings and was constantly monitoring for any sign of change or warning from my guides that we were in harm's way. We were after all, in the most active area of the house which wasn't an ideal situation.

She goes on to say, *'So many time's I'd tried to break free from this spell to prevent the inevitable from happening. The more I fought back, the more I would feel a tightening around my neck, like an invisible tourniquet. I've tried to scream. My mouth opens, but nothing comes out. I feel something like hands move all over my body, grabbing at my breasts and pulling at my legs. I'm so ashamed. When I first started to experience this, believe it or not, I was consensual as I actually thought it was my husband. You know when you are in that sleepy dreamy state and not quite awake, but once I was aware... Oh my God! How do you get your head around that? I even started reciting the Lord's Prayer over and over in my head as a form of blocking it out.'*

I'd asked her, *'Are you religious?'*

Brenda replied: *'I'm not religious, but I had to turn to something. When you experience something like this happening to you, you don't know what to do. I learnt the Lord's Prayer and when the attack was happening to me I kept praying, with my eyes closed, and I would remove myself from my body and of what was really happening. I concentrated all my efforts and energy on the verses until I felt the weight lifting from my chest, and then I knew it was over. It never lasted long but it seemed to last forever.'*

Brenda was holding her emotions together, but you could see the pain. *'After each attack, I'd feel disgusted. I'd jump out of bed and shower, scrubbing away at my body, examining myself for any physical signs of rape.'*

'Is there any evidence?' I asked, *'Was David aware of any of this?'*

I could see Brenda was uncomfortable when she stated, *'There was none other than a few fingertip bruises around my neck and inner thighs. I did try and tell David the first time I experienced an attack, but he didn't take me seriously and thought I had an overactive imagination. So, I kept quiet about it.'* It was clear David had struggled to believe what was happening.

As to show me an example, Brenda recounted that on one occasion whilst sitting downstairs in the lounge, entertaining their two guests, a loud bang was heard coming from above. They listened as heavy footsteps moved from one corner of the ceiling to the other. *'All of us were looking up towards the ceiling tracing with our eyes the direction of the sound. David and our friend Alan thought it must be an intruder and both ran upstairs.'* Brenda knew from the moment the door hit the wall it wasn't an intruder. In fact, I believe she would have preferred if it was. She knew exactly what it was. *'Though alarmed, Joan and I remained downstairs listening. After checking all the bedrooms, they shouted down that no one was up there. They came downstairs and said the only thing they could see was an indentation mark on the wall, in the master bedroom. David and Alan assumed the dent must have been the noise we heard when the door had been slammed open. If there was an intruder, they're gone now.'*

It was clear Brenda felt isolated and withdrawn. She wasn't feeling comfortable with sharing her plight. I needed to keep her talking and asked, *'How often did the visits occur?'*

She told me, *'The night visits continued in the same vein, but they had recently increased to an average of twice a week.'* With her husband not believing her after so many incidents, it was no wonder she struggled to open up to anyone about what was happening. In hindsight, away from the house, thinking about all the signs, I wondered why the penny hadn't dropped sooner for David. Why didn't he realise that they were dealing with something unnatural to this earth?

I then asked her to do something that I knew would be very difficult for her to do, *'Can you please describe the attack that stands out in your mind?'* This type of information is very important to building the psychic profile and understanding the characteristics, temperament and attack style of the entity.

She took a deep breath, summoning up all her courage and said, *'One night whilst sitting up reading, the bedroom door suddenly flung wide open. I was alert and wide awake. I looked over at David who was snoring beside me, deep in sleep. I called out his name, but he didn't answer. I screamed his name and prodded him hard, but still, he didn't move. I was fretful, as I sensed the room was closing in on me with that familiar sensation I always feel just prior to an attack. The room took on that same icy chill. I bent my head over onto David's chest to hear if his heart was still beating. I thought he was dead.'*

With a slight pause, she continued, *'Whilst bent over David, a great force threw me up into the air and back down roughly onto my back. It felt like an invisible pair of hands had just grabbed me like a rag doll and pinned me down on the bed. I couldn't move. A heavy weight was pressing down on me, and I could feel everything. His fingers were poking and prodding me. It was disgusting. He was assaulting me, and I was literally powerless to fight back.'*

'I could only move my eyes. My mind was intact, and I was very much aware of my surroundings. I looked down at myself; clearly seeing my body move to that of touch. I felt sick with fear. I was being raped by an invisible force. Once it was over, David only stirred. I was so angry with him for not waking up to protect me. I'd never felt so isolated and alone.' With a look of anguish, Brenda's facial expression matched her story.

'I jumped out of bed and ran into the shower scrubbing my body trying to wash the filth away.' She gestured the scrubbing motion with her hands demonstrating her desperation to remove even the tiniest reminder of what had happened. *'I was shocked to notice on my breasts were several small bruises and strange raised indentations marks that had appeared on my inner thighs. They resembled teeth marks. My back felt very sore, so I turned to look at my reflection in the mirror and could see several bright red welt marks were appearing. Although in discomfort, I ran from the shower half crying and half laughing with relief. I shook David violently to wake him. He woke up startled and oblivious to what had just occurred. I showed him the marks on my body. He was shocked. He could clearly make out the teeth marks on each leg and welts on my back.'*

As Brenda got through the most difficult part of her story, I could see her body and facial expression had started to relax. She continued, *'The following morning, David added more security. He put a CCTV camera facing the front and back entrance of our house and another in our bedroom. This heightened security did give us some peace of mind. I felt he was at least listening to me, although I knew he was still struggling to get his head around the full scale of what was exactly happening to me.'*

I wanted to keep the momentum going and moved the conversation onto her latest attack. Several weeks had passed without an incident. She thought that maybe the assaults had stopped as quickly as they had begun, but then Brenda told me, *'My last attack happened only a few days ago. David was lying next to me in bed, asleep, when the atmosphere in the room suddenly changed; just as it had done on so many other occasions. The room temperature dropped dramatically.'* This was a familiar sign something was about to happen. *'I was determined to fight and not be a victim. I'd screamed for David to wake up. Thankfully, this time, he did!'*

A slight tremor ran through her body. *'The familiar tingling sensation, like mild electric shocks, had started to creep around my ankles and was travelling up both shins. I remember frantically kicking in the hope of keeping control over my legs. A warm breath blew across my face at very close range. It stunk of stale alcohol and cigarettes.'*

'I jumped up out of bed swiping at the air in front of me, brushing the smell away from my face. David also leapt out of bed, alert and ready for whatever fate we had in store. Suddenly, something grabbed me with aggression pinning me against the wall. My feet couldn't touch the ground, and it was trying to open my legs while I was frantically fighting back. David's expression, in his wild fearful eyes, was one of shock and disbelief. He was seeing it all. The look on his face will forever be with me.'

'David lunged forward trying to get to me and protect me from this invisible monster. In a shaky voice, he was screaming at the entity "Leave her alone!" I was horrified as David was pulled backwards, away from me. Then, his body started to rise. It was levitating several inches into the air before he was thrown like a paper plane, to the far side of the bed. He slammed hard into the wall hitting his back; momentarily winding him. His face held that look of disbelief of what he was experiencing. He crumbled like a broken man and began to cry, not out of pain but out of desperation. He kept repeating "I didn't believe you, I didn't believe you!" I knew he felt powerless. He was out of his depth.'

'David was beside himself. He kept rewinding the tape over and over, but nothing had been captured on the CCTV. This attack was by far the most violent to date. We were both so scared, we didn't dare go to sleep just in case it should return.'

'We decided to sleep downstairs on our pull-out sofa bed in the lounge. We only slept lightly. Both of us were becoming exhausted and drained. David would test the camera for any images night after

night, but nothing was captured. We felt like prisoners in our own home, confined to the relative safety of the downstairs.'

I could see the story was taking it out of her, but she bravely went on, *'We kept a lamp on constantly throughout the night. On this night, it turned itself off, leaving the room in total darkness. David immediately sprang into action and turned on the overhead light. It came on for seconds only, before going out.'*

'We thought there must be a power cut. The circuit breaker is located at the back of the house in the utility room. Both of us, hand in hand and armed with torches, made our way through the darkness. When we got there, no switches had been triggered. There was no apparent reason for the power loss. David was confused as there wasn't even a power failure alarm to show that the electricity in the house had been lost.'

'We got back to the lounge and instantly noticed that our blankets had been neatly folded like a tower with our pillows placed on top! This freaked us both out so much! We grabbed the keys and couldn't get out of the house quick enough.'

'We no longer felt safe in our own home and had decided to stay at a hotel for the night. We needed to think about our next course of action.' Brenda was slightly shaking her head as if in disbelief of the position they were in. *'We were running away, and David hated that fact. On returning the following day, the blankets were still neatly folded with pillows placed on the top… and the lamp was on! That was it. I made up my mind and told David I wanted to leave this house. I knew he didn't want to move as too much of his time and effort had gone into it. He had to admit he was not happy either and could see no other alternative but to sell up.'*

Brenda and David went to see their friends of many years, Joan and Alan. Over dinner, they revealed their extraordinary yet horrifying experiences leaving Joan and Alan transfixed. They knew David wasn't one to exaggerate. They followed his every word as he told them of the event after event in brutal detail.

Joan mentioned she may be able to help as one of her associates, from a WI group, had experienced some physical phenomena and believed it had been sorted out. This is how I'd become involved. I was the investigator in Joan's friend's case.

I was intrigued to get to the bottom of this and find out who, or what was making Brenda's life hell.

On the day of the spiritual cleanse, I'd checked that the CCTV camera was running and advised everyone else to remain downstairs and not to come upstairs, no matter what they may hear. My video camera was already placed on a tripod positioned at the foot of the bed in the master bedroom. With all my technical checks complete, I was ready to start.

Joan and Alan were in attendance downstairs for moral support. It was around 12.45am when I laid down on top of Brenda's side of the master bed. Tuning into my guides, as in mental mediumship, I asked them to draw close to me with their protective light. Following my ritual to confirm a deep grounding and protection, I then asked that my clearance guides were at hand, ready to intercept the entity and aid him into the light.

After a few moments, with my eyes closed, I'd become aware of a severe drop-in room temperature. Brenda warned me about this, as this is how the visits always began. I opened my eyes to grab a neatly folded blanket that was placed at the foot of the bed. I decided to use it to keep myself warm from the now very chilly room. It got so cold, my face was frozen to the touch. I pulled the hood of my tracksuit over my head, tugging hard on the strings for a snug fit to try and get that little bit more warmth and comfort.

My eyes were now adjusted to the dimness of the room. Looking around me, I took note of where everything was placed. The room took on an eerie deafening silence. I was eagerly anticipating when the action would start and knew this was just the build-up. The red pinprick of light, coming from the video camera, confirmed in my mind that the camera was still recording.

Moments passed when I began to feel a familiar sensation to my right-hand side. An indication that my protector had joined me. Standing proud, holding his decorative tribal shield and spear, with an image of almost 7ft tall, lean but muscular black frame, Zulu is my spiritual Protector guide who protects me both physically and spiritually from harm. He makes an intimidating sight as he has been physically witnessed several times by others who have been present, during other encounters. When he makes an appearance, I know things are going to get heavy. Though ever so powerful, he will not intervene until I call him to do so.

Continuing to draw in even closer to me, Zulu was empowering me with great confidence. It was being made clear to me the entity wouldn't go without a fight. This would no longer be a cleanse. My Clearance guides wouldn't be able to aid the entity into the light until it was restrained. The spirit entity, against its will, would have to be physically removed.

No noise could be heard coming from downstairs. I wondered if they too must have been doing the same and listening for any sounds coming from me, above them. The room temperature had started to drop again, making it a little uncomfortable with warm breath escaping from my mouth as I exhaled. I was aware of a subtle change to the vibration and atmosphere around me. The air seemed condensed. It made my breathing a little more laboured.

I knew it wasn't going to be too long now before I came face to face with the Entity. The adrenaline began to rush through my body, a process I go through in preparation for battle. I was ready for his visit and all that he had to offer.

With an almighty thud, the door flew open. This was my first sight at how powerful this entity truly was. A shaft of light streamed in from the lamp, placed in the corridor. I glanced up at the CCTV, preying it was capturing this. A distinctive rotting aroma of ectoplasm began to fill the room. Knowing that the physical spirit manifestation was close, I'd reinforced my protection of my aura to avoid the entity tapping in and gaining control over me both spiritually and physically.

I could feel him trying to invade my auric space. He was trying to take my energy from me and use it as his own. I could actually feel his frustration growing as he knew something was wrong. Fighting his way closer to me, I could feel his breath blowing past my face along with the sensation of him sniffing me, just like a predatory animal.

Sitting bolt upright, with my back pressed hard against the headboard, I made sure he couldn't surprise me with an attack from behind. The pinprick of red light had disappeared. I'd hoped the batteries had not died and wondered if he had been the cause, draining everything he could for energy.

Speaking out loud, with a raised voice, I told him *'You are not invited here! You must leave. I'm not afraid of you!'* A horrible deep growling sound came from mid-air. The words, *'she's mine, she's mine'* echoed within the room.

The following took place over seconds…

In my peripheral view, the bedside cabinet had the slightest of moves to catch my attention. As I turned my head slightly toward the cabinet, it was thrust up at me. I ducked quickly toward the middle of the bed, narrowly escaping, as it crashed into the adjacent wall. This was only a decoy to try and take my attention and concentration away from him. I forcefully raised my voice asking, *'You need to leave. You aren't invited here!'* I'd started to pray out loud and called for peace to be restored to this dwelling. The banging intensified in volume, trying to drown out my words. Loud thuds seemed to resonate from every direction with pictures that had been hanging on the wall being dislodged and thrown onto the ground. The loud bangs were all around me, so intense that I wanted to cover my ears. I raised my voice to be heard over the sound of destruction.

The entity lunged forward to physically attack me. I could feel heaviness upon my chest. He was trying to strangle me as I continued to pray aloud. Loud bangs came from within the Chester-drawers which stood on the other side of the bedroom. Each drawer began to fall forwards, releasing themselves from their housing. Their contents were being sprawled all over the floor. Perfumes and ornaments, placed on top of units, were flying at me through the air. The entity was throwing a tantrum, and we both knew he was using up vital energy with this physical outburst.

With his hands still at my throat, trying to seal my silence, this entity was getting far too close for comfort. I mentally called Zulu in, and with no nonsense, the pressure was released. Within less than a second, peace was restored to the room. I knew Zulu had him under control, and I was safe.

My Clearance guides could now come in. I asked them to intervene at this stage to assist the entity into the light. My Rescue guide, Nun Sister Francis, conducts this part of the cleanse as my Zulu is my Protector guide only. I understand from my learnings that the entity will be taken through a form of counselling, where he will learn to understand and come to terms with his conditioning.

Warmth seemed to slowly ebb back around me. As my eyes scanned around, I could see the room was trashed. Broken table lamps and fragments of bedside cabinets were scattered. Clothes and personal items were strewn across the floor. I waited and listened... nothing could be heard!

I'd asked my guides *'Who is it, what is his name?'* They replied *'Brian.'* They gave me a briefing as to why this happened and what Brian wanted.

I got up and turned on the overhead light. The first thing I'd noticed was that the tripod had been deliberately turned around to face the brick wall.

Going downstairs, gasping for a cup of coffee, they were all sitting on the edge of their seats, as I'd entered the lounge. Everyone jumped up talking at the same time, asking if I was ok and what happened? After I reassured them I was fine, and the entity was gone, I just needed a moment to sit down for a second as I had just used a serious amount of physical energy.

I got served a delicious victory cup of coffee. After having a few good sips and getting some energy back, I was ready to relay what had transpired and passed on the information my guides had revealed to me.

The Entities name was Brian. He believed Brenda to have been his own wife. I went on to explain that although his physical body was discarded, his soul essence had lived on. Brian had been the previous owner of the farm and still walked the land, refusing to relinquish his hold.

I'd stayed the rest of the evening to give confidence to them that all was clear. Joan and Alan were also staying the night and went off to their respective guest room. David & Brenda decided to finish the night in the lounge and when confident, would move back into their bedroom. Everything stayed quiet. The night had gone without further incident. At this point, I didn't know if David & Brenda would ever use the Master bedroom again after all that had happened.

Over breakfast, Brenda had asked me, *'Is it possible that negative energies can attach themselves to objects?'* I'd explained this was possible. Mediums have the ability to check for negativity by feeling the vibration when touching the object. This is known as psychometry. I asked her why she asked such a question.

She went out of the room and returned with two porcelain clowns. They were around three-foot-tall with movable limbs. Both were dressed in vibrant colours with grotesque expressions upon their faces. *'These were a gift to David from his first wife. He doesn't want to part with them, but they give me the creeps. Can you check them for negative energy?'*

I could see, deep in her heart, she wanted me to convey that they held a negative charge, giving her a cause to get rid of them. I psychometrised both clowns and found they did hold a residue but nothing too bad and certainly not attributed to the physical phenomena they had been experiencing. Knowing she didn't want to hear this bit of information, I still had to be honest. Just then, David walked back into the room frowning, when he saw me holding the clowns over my lap and asked, *'What's up?'*

Looking up at Brenda, I'd left it for her to fill him in. She told him *'Objects can hold a negative current, and these two clowns do, we have been advised to get rid of them.'* She glanced me a quick pleading look. David was confused and needed clarification from me if this was the case. I just nodded and confirmed that objects can hold a negative current, and these in fact did. Brenda interrupted me by saying *'We must get shot of them as soon as possible.'* He reluctantly nodded, saying he would do it later that day.

I looked over to David and asked, *'Was anything captured on the CCTV?'* He replied *'There was something there, but I couldn't make it out. It looks like a mass of black smoke was right next to you, when you were lying on the bed. No other footage was captured. Most of the images were distorted.'*

Later that evening, Brenda called me with alarm in her voice. I was dreading what she was about to say. What she explained to me was a real mystery, and one I cannot fathom to this day.

'Not long after you left, I had put the two clowns in a black sack, and I distinctly remember securing it with a double knot. We had to make an errand to the local DIY store to collect two internal doors, so we took the tail truck to collect them.'

'I threw the sack into the back of the truck. David was already seated in the driving seat, engine running ready to go. We went to the dump on route to the DIY store. I witnessed David throwing the sack into the dump. The truck was empty when we placed the doors into the back.'

'It was whilst driving into our lane, near our home, that David and I saw it… The clown was just sitting there on the road sign! He was propped up by a twig which had grown up behind the sign. I am sure his expression held a smug look.'

Joan had popped back later that night to check in on them. Brenda relayed the bizarre events to her. Joan said she didn't see anything on the sign as she drove in. Brenda questioned her a number of times of which Joan kept reassuring her nothing was there.

Receiving an update from Brenda a few days later, she told me all was quiet, with no visitations at all. They were back in their bedroom, and life seemed to be slowly getting back to normal.

She informed me of a conversation they had had with their neighbours, who had made David very welcome to the hamlet when he first moved in. They revealed they had known Brian, as he was the previous owner of the farm that David and Brenda lived in.

Brian was not a nice character; a bully who was physically abusive to his wife Brenda, especially when he had been drinking. Before his death, Brian and Brenda were separated with Brenda living in the Farmhouse and Brian living in the outbuilding. He was prosecuted for assaulting her during one of his outbursts and had a court enforcement order placed upon him to keep his distance from her.

Summary:
It is my feeling that when David extended the farmhouse, connecting it to the outbuilding, he had unknowingly brought Brain back into the home. The building work that was carried out could also be contributed to stimulating

spiritual activity. His strong emotion of jealousy was why he had remained earthbound. The name 'Brenda' was key believing David's wife to be his own. He was hell-bent on being involved in her life as he never got over her rejection of him in his lifetime.

This event was a result of Brian having a clear case of mistaken identity.

The house was checked over for any plausible explanations that could have caused the bluebottle phenomenon. Nothing was found. The analysis report, from the Pest Control Centre, had revealed the cause of death as being of natural causes. There was no further outbreak of fly infestation.

Neither clown was ever seen again!

Chapter 2
MISSING

It is estimated that on average 275,000 people are reported as missing each year. Though missing persons tracing agencies provide a service of support and advice for loved ones, for the majority of cases, there can't be any relief until the individuals are found. Day after day, families wait for word that their loved ones are safe. Sometimes, those days turn into years, with each day becoming an agonising and unbearable wait.

Eddie had been missing for 6 years at the time I was asked to help. Eddie's aunt Minnie had contacted me. She wanted to have a sitting with me in regard to her missing nephew. Her hope was that I may be able to throw some light onto what has happened to him.

I've never attempted a case like this and I wasn't sure if she had contacted the right person. For whatever reason, unknown to me, she wanted me to at least try.

Eddie's profile details were on several missing person's bureaus. To date, his whereabouts are still unknown because his body has never been found. His mobile phone and bank account had not been used after his disappearance. There haven't been any sightings of Eddie, nor has any further detail been revealed around the case.

On the day of the sitting I knew expectations were high. I stood at Minnie's front door. I was nervous. This was going to be a new experience and I didn't know how it would unfold or what would be asked of me as a medium. Would I have the right tools and knowledge to get the answers Minnie so desperately wanted?

The pressure was immense. Minnie opened the door and welcomed me into her home with a warm embrace.

We entered a very small room putting us in very close proximity to each other. I was still downloading details about the case and trying to find my feet.

Minnie was very keen to start, but I was feeling a little claustrophobic. I asked Minnie, *'Do you have a picture of Eddie I could use to make a connection?'* Minnie provided a photo of two men standing side by side. She pointed out which one was Eddie and made no reference to the other man.

I asked if I could have a cup of coffee to create some physical space and give myself some time to get my bearings. By the time Minnie returned with a cup of coffee, I had received some information from my guides while looking at Eddie's picture. I had taken some notes and was ready to start. I also asked and was given permission for the session to be recorded. There are several reasons I like to record my paranormal and missing cases. The main two reasons are for proof of what I'd said and to see if any EVP had occurred during the session that we wouldn't have heard. One other reason, that might seem odd to some, is that once I give the information, I generally forget about it. The requirement to retain such information isn't necessary as the message is for the sitter as opposed to me.

The downloads I receive from my guides are not complete. They are merely fragments and pieces of a puzzle that I must translate and piece together. These fragments can consist of random names and dates that will somehow come together to become a picture relevant to the reading. More pieces of the puzzle are always added during the reading. It takes time to develop the story and all you can do as a medium is to start with the information you have. Even though this was a missing person's case, the reading was very much in line with my normal work giving me much needed confidence.

I was looking deep into the eyes of Eddie's photo when a rush of emotion came over me. A female in spirit had come forward identifying herself as Minnie's mother. She provided how she had passed along with some personal memories to validate who she was. This was followed with a gentleman coming forward saying he was Minnie's father. He was drawing my attention to the bookcase to the side of me. He said, *'There's a book on the shelf that I had written in.'* I told Minnie, *'I have your father here. He is drawing my attention to a book that holds his signature.'* She remembered the book well and grabbed it off the shelf. Flipping the book to reveal the front cover, she showed me where he had written a personal message to her and signed his signature, validating their bond.

Her family were providing many messages, but none of the messages were about Eddie. Minnie shifted to the edge of her seat, leaning forward with intent in her eye. She asked, *'Is Eddie with them? Has he passed?'* I asked the question, as she put it to me, out loud to spirit. The response was that he wasn't with them.

Minnie let out a sigh of relief, which made me feel very uneasy. This question was only one of many that needed to be asked. We'd only established that he wasn't with the family in the white light. This didn't establish he was alive. Even though I didn't have experience in this type of work, the uneasy feeling I was receiving was telling me that something wasn't right. As my connection was a strong link, I continued.

With each family connection that came through, they were divulging common information that you would hear in any other reading. Though it was personal information for Minnie and it gave her some warmth, it wasn't the information she was desperate for.

It was strange how there was no mention from any of them concerning Eddie's whereabouts. Minnie was frowning, trying to make sense of the information she was receiving, but confused at not receiving any detail about Eddie in any way.

She asked me again to ask them if they had information about what happened to Eddie. The reply was, *'He is not with us.'* The thought had crossed my mind, could this mean that he was alive? Was he living somewhere? Didn't he want to be found? Why was the vibration I was feeling not aligned with what they were saying? I felt this meant that there was more to be revealed.

I continued with the reading. Two gentlemen had come through together, side by side. The elder of the two identified himself as Minnie's maternal grandfather. He was a beautiful link. He talked about the disappearance of his gold watch, a Rolex, from his home. Minnie remembered the incident and commented, *'It had never been found.'* Her grandfather said, *'Eddie took it.'* He wanted her to know that he understood the situation and holds no malice or blame towards him.

He explained to Minnie that from spirit side he can see the things that he could not whilst on the earth plane. He continued to say that Eddie had sold it to gain money to purchase his newly formed drug habit. Minnie was shocked to have been informed of this knowledge but not of the fact of the drug addiction. She said she had heard he'd got himself involved with a new group of lads who were into drugs.

The other spirit gentleman came forward to connect with me.

His vibration was very different. Every spirit connection radiates a different vibration, capturing their personality and emotional state. He showed me through mental mediumship an image of him with his head bent down held in his hands. A feeling of desperation and oppression came over me. I asked for validation as to whom he was and if he had a message for Minnie. In describing his look and of the nature of his passing from a massive heart attack, she instantly knew who it was and broke down, *'Aye, it's my Brother, Eddie's Dad.'*

He was the other gentleman in the picture, standing beside Eddie. She told me he had died two years after Eddie's disappearance. A few private words were shared between them.

Images continued playing out within my mind. I was shown a white van, of which she confirmed was his. She told me he would spend all day and night just driving around, putting up posters and asking everyone if they had seen him. Through her tears, she asked him, *'Is Eddie with you?'* I was given the same reply, *'No, he isn't.'*

Minnie was now crying from desperation. She told me the doctors believed her brother had died of a broken heart. His grief was too much to bear.

The emotion was proving too much for me and was weakening my connection. I had to ask my guides to remove the emotional aspect to keep a strong connection. Personal emotion must be kept under control during a reading as it can distort how the medium translates the information coming through, as it would come from a place of avoiding pain as opposed to its true translation as they want it presented. The best mediums give messages the way they are received without putting their own spin on it. Saying this, subjects such as health and death do require tact.

I took a moment and had a sip of my coffee. I didn't want to break my connection entirely, but I needed that time to recompose my thoughts. I used Eddie's picture to refocus my intention and it was whilst looking at Eddie, that in my mind's eye, he had moved and became animated. I saw him hold up a keyring with two keys upon it. He was smiling broadly. I mentioned to Minnie of my vision, she smiled and said, *'aye, he passed his driving test the day that picture was taken.'* It was also his 21st Birthday, it's the last picture ever taken of him.

Minnie was curious to know what I had written in my notes. I mentioned several Christian names and a nickname of another. Minnie shuddered as she instantly recognised the names. *'Go on,'* she said, shuffling further to the edge of the seat. Minnie instantly recognised a female's name as Eddie's girlfriend. I felt her name was separate to that of the other males, but at this stage I did not know why.

Minnie asked again, *'Do they know where Eddie is? Do they have information?'* I was drawn back to the energy of the male's nickname and felt he was an unsavoury character. I was shown a vision in my mind of the bars of a prison cell. I asked Minnie if she knew of this guy. She replied, *'Aye I do, he's a bad one. Always been in trouble. The last I heard he was in prison serving a manslaughter sentence. He comes from bad stock. He was a thug in a drug syndicate ring.'*

I asked, *'Do you know if Eddie connected with him?'* Minnie replied, *'Aye he did, he was ore struck wanted to be in his gang, silly lad.'* I felt he had knowledge of what happened to Eddie but he wouldn't divulge what he knew.

Picking up Eddie's picture, I looked deep in his eyes again, but this time I became at one with him. In my mind, I saw him wearing a black zip-up puffer style jacket made of a nylon type material and snow-white trainers. Minnie confirmed this was the jacket and trainers he received for his birthday. These were the clothes he was last seen wearing, prior to his disappearance. She also mentioned he had changed into them as soon as he'd unwrapped them.
With urgency in her voice, she asked, *'Who's telling you this information? Is it him? Has he passed?'* Her voice was very emotional and strained. In all honesty, I could not tell her if it was him showing me or my guides. This was a first-time for me. I had never experienced this form of communication before.

I'd become a little uneasy as the image continued to unfold akin to watching a cinema clip within my mind as if recalling my own memory, facts, and emotions. I was thankful for the tape machine recording my running commentary.

This was such an odd experience that I had to check with my guides to make sure it was okay to continue. I was reassured it was okay so carried on providing any information that came through, making sure I spoke loud enough for the recorder to capture each bit of detail. I stayed mindful of relaying the message just as it was received. Similar to an answering machine, without emotion.

I was aware of my own voice questioning, *'What do you see? Where are we?'* At this point, I didn't know to whom I was asking the question.

I mentally received an image of a blue wooden front door and what sounded like two males who were angry and having a heated argument. I was so into the vision, that when I heard a door slamming harshly (in my mind), it startled me, and I jumped out of my seat. I was then taken to a clear visual image of looking down an uneven grey cobblestone street. I physically felt the sensation of walking and described what I could see on my journey. I trusted my connection, so continued with this style of spirit projection.

A low wall, about knee height, came into view. It was just to my left. Behind it, stood a large block of flats, four levels high. To my right, I saw an image of two corner shops. It was at this point that Minnie confirmed, *'Aye that's the corner bakers shop adjoined to the newsagents.'* I asked, *'Do you recognise the flats I'm referring to?'* She asked me, *'Can you see the name of the road?'* The name 'Shakespeare' was written upon a sign. Minnie, with a look of surprise had encouraged me to keep the connection going.

The images continued to download into my mind. I could smell the distinctive aroma of cigarette smoke. It was so strong that I'd opened my eyes to see if Minnie had lit up a cigarette. Of course, she hadn't.

I then heard the unmistakable sound of a billiard cue, as it met with the ball. I knew I was in a smoke-filled billiard room. Minnie interjected, *'aye I recognise what you say. I know the area you talk about.'* She became very excited as she could identify and confirm all that was coming through. Minnie was tracing my journey step by step. I had never been to this location in my life, but luckily Minnie knew it very well.

Growing in confidence, I asked my guides to show me more. I felt we were now following a trail. I began to experience feelings and have thoughts of which were not my own. My visual connection became 3D with a panoramic view of all that surrounded me. I could see all their faces. It was mainly men, but there was one female face that stood out. She was young, blonde and of slim build. I knew she was connected in some emotional way to Eddie and had knowingly withheld some knowledge.

My vision had taken me outside once again. It was dusk. The air was cold. I had the sensation of walking alone at great speed. My heart was beginning to race with a feeling of heightened anxiety. I was meeting someone and had felt nervous. I had come off the road and followed a pathway to my right. This lead me onto a grass bank, of which widened onto a vastness of open land.

There was no visible lighting provided by street lamps or the houses nearby. My footsteps had become quietened by the softness of the ground beneath me. Tall trees and bushes were to the left of my vision and I became aware of an expanse of water to my right.

As I looked in more detail, the moon had highlighted a bridge with high arches beneath its structure. The bridge crossed a fast running river. I could hear the water lapping against its edge. Within my mind, I heard a male's voice and my heart quickened. A real fear had overcome me. My mouth became very dry.

Minnie was rooted to the spot eager for me to continue. I was feeling a little agitated and wanted to close the sitting or at least to have a break. I wondered if I would be able to reconnect again if I did. At this point, I wasn't sure if I even wanted to. I was getting deep into a situation where I had never ventured before. I still had concern that I hadn't received confirmation as to whom I was actually connected with. Before I had time to make that decision, my mind took on a frenzy of images. I continued to pass on the details to Minnie that were coming through to me. It was if they didn't want to give me a chance to stop.

I saw a group of Asian males of differing ages with one character standing out from the others. I sensed real fear and knew great danger laid ahead. The face of one of the Asian men seemed to encompass the whole of my mind. His features were so clear and distinctive. I knew he meant malice.

It was whilst I was concentrating on his face that I physically experienced a great pain, to the back of my neck. I remember consciously putting my hands to my head, the pain momentarily taking my breath away. There were raised voices and tensions were high. A fight had broken out. The Asian guy was more muscular toned and physically stronger in stature had lunged towards another male. The other male was Eddie.

As the violent conflict was revealing itself to me, it was clear to see that Eddie wasn't a match for him. From a shimmer of moonlight, I could see the glimpse of a long knife blade. During his turmoil, Eddie was grabbed. I could see the knife being forcibly rammed into his back. 'Oh no!' I cried out, hearing my own voice. Upon opening my eyes, I saw Minnie's raised hands over her face. She was in shock.

Eddie fell forward and then laid there motionless. I saw the others in the group had formed a circle surrounding him. I could see his white trainers illuminated by the moonlight as he rolled down the river bank. Everything went quiet. I felt sick to my stomach. The next thing I heard was a splash of water. The image within my mind was broken by the howling sound of what could be best described as a wounded animal, shrieking out in pain. It was Minnie. I was not happy to continue anymore with this link.

Minnie asked, *'Is he dead? Was that how he had met his end?'* I questioned everything and wondered myself. How could it be that if I had witnessed Eddie's murder, then why wasn't he with his father and family members in spirit?

The spirit connection previously made with Minnie's mother had returned. She wanted me to ask Minnie about her recent purchase, a calendar. Minnie was shocked to hear of this because she had confirmed she had not long come back from a short stay away and had been buying Christmas presents. She had indeed bought a yearly calendar for a friend. The calendar was still in its sealed wrapping. She went in search of her purchase. Her mother had asked her to break the seal and go to the month of April.

Minnie remarked, as she unwrapped the calendar, this was the month Eddie disappeared. I was unsure where this information was leading. The calendar depicted well-known pictures throughout the months of the locations she had recently visited. The image for the month of April, was the exact drawing I had scribbled on my notes at the beginning of our meeting. It was of a bridge, with arches beneath its structure. It crossed the river Tay in Dundee. I had never visited this region and had no prior knowledge of this bridge.

A shudder ran through me on the revelation of the picture. Holding up my drawing and placing it side by side to the calendar picture, it was undeniably the same place. My scribbled notes revealed Eddie lay at the water's edge in the River Tay, deep in the silt, near to the structure of the first arch.

Minnie informed me that she generally selected calendars with animals but had felt drawn to this one. I had realised my link from spirit was from Eddie himself.

He had shared his images with me of the last day he was alive and met his demise. With the last bit of my energy still available, I wanted to tune into his energy once again. I wanted to ask him if he was aware of his father's passing. I asked for assistance from my guides to locate Eddie's father. I was going to try, with the help of my guides, to connect their souls.

Once again, in my mind, I instantly recognised the location I was being shown. It was the spot where Eddie had fallen and lost his life. I had asked Minnie's mother to connect once again with me and to bring forward her son, Eddie's father. A few moments had passed when I could clearly see Eddie standing beside the water's edge. A tall being, angelic in form, accompanied Eddie, casting his beautiful light upon him.

Moments passed before he was joined with his father. It was so beautiful to see them reunited and embracing each other. father & son had stood together in each other's arms.

Eddie turned and looked in my direction. He smiled and nodded his gratification for reuniting him with his father and for helping him fully crossover.

Minnie had felt a sense of relief and closure, at least to this point. I explained to Minnie that they were not able to connect in spirit because they were in different planes of existence and thus didn't know of each other's demise.

Eddie, due to his traumatic passing had caused him to remain earthbound. His soul energy lingered in the physical world, even after his physical existence ended. He didn't make the transition to the other side. Many reasons can cause this such as unfinished business, fear or a sudden violent death.

A few weeks later, Minnie contact me. She had checked the information that had come through from the sitting. She contacted Eddie's girlfriend as her family still resided in Dundee. His girlfriend said that on the night of his disappearance, she felt that she must have been one of the last people to have seen him. She also confirmed he had met up with his new group of undesirables, the druggies she called them. They were having a meeting about something, of which she was not involved in. She said she tried to dissuade him from having anything to do with them.

She saw Eddie leave the hall on his own and said, *'He had something to do. He looked really nervous, but he said that he would call me later that night.'* Shortly after, the gang had left the hall together. This was the account she told the police. This was the last time she had heard or seen anything of Eddie.

She admitted that she didn't divulge to the Police all that she had overheard as she had feared for her safety. It was Eddie's first drug run for the gang and the gang had informed him that they would have his back.

During my time working on this case, a small independent film company wanted to be involved in some of my cases. Minnie had given her permission and allowed them to listen to the tape recording.

They had asked her for the full postal address of where Eddie was living at the time of his disappearance. I sat beside the crew as they logged on to 'Google Earth' and typed in the address. I was interested to see the comparison. The little gingerbread man figure was ready for instructions. They had step by step followed the route I spoke of, as per the tape recording.

They began at Eddie's address the one with a blue door and noted the grey cobbled road within the image. The name of Shakespeare could be clearly seen on the road sign where the block of flats was situated just behind the small wall. The two shops Eddie described on the corner of the road, had come into view.

They crew continued to follow the arrow straight ahead where further up the road, the sign of the billiard hall hung above the building.

Eddie had imparted these images within my mind of his last physical journey.

Summary:
In some cases where individuals who have been murdered may feel they cannot move from those feelings of anger and sadness and will stay earthbound to their human life not yet willing to accept their transformation into spirit.

It was wonderful to be reassured that after so many years of grief for the family, that Eddie was reunited once more with his loved ones.

Chapter 3

TRAPPED

The walls had been draped with expensive damask wallpaper, which complemented the elaborate mirrors and chandeliers, creating an ambience of elegance. This was perfect for a high-end hair and beauty salon. This beautiful property has undoubtedly hosted a variety of different businesses throughout its years and has its own story to tell.

Ian is the proprietor of this three storied, 18th century, building that stands proudly in a popular Hertfordshire market square. He invested a lot of time and money into rejuvenating this old building, turning his dream into a reality. He was referred to me by one of his customers who knew of my work.

My initial telephone conversation with Ian went on a lot longer than I normally like. I prefer to limit my exposure to the detail so that I can get non-opinionated views from my guides on what is happening. This conversation was an exception to my normal rule. I didn't mind as I felt no one is in any urgent danger.

Ian began with telling me of one of his own experiences, '*I needed to catch up on some paperwork and remained in the salon late one evening. All the staff had left for the day. I'd felt a sensation that I wasn't alone. I was being watched. When I looked up, I noticed several dark shadows silhouetted upon the walls. They varied in height. It resembled a gathering of people. I could hear whispering voices at close range, but I couldn't decipher what was being said.*'

'*My customers are reporting seeing images reflected in the mirror, like shadow people, standing behind them,*' he stated. Even the music they play in the background was being disrupted. Some customers were saying it was EVP (Electronic Voice Phenomena) caused by ghosts. All the electrical items, like hairdryers and trimmers, turn themselves on and off at will. You could hear the concern in his voice as Ian continued, *'At first, it was taken light-hearted, but now my customers are becoming uncomfortable and even frightened by the strange experiences. They aren't coming back.'*

Ian is generally the first person to open the salon in the morning. On one occasion, he found the pyramid display of used hair products strewn all over the salon floor. His business cards were spread in a neat display across the reception desk. While he was cleaning up the business cards and placing them back into their container, he said, *'I saw a full head to toe apparition of a child watching me.'* It is quite unusual to see a full head to toe apparition. Most are lucky when they get to see a portion of the body or a silhouette. Ian continued, *'I felt they knew I could see them. I was stunned and felt like a rabbit in headlights.'*

'Over the months the increase in poltergeist activity has heightened with more customers witnessing hairbrushes, scissors and implements being thrown, from one side of the salon to the other when there had been no one else present.' I asked if he felt anyone was in danger of getting hurt during these incidents. He replied *I couldn't say. My staff are also reporting seeing the cupboard doors and drawers, in the kitchen, open by themselves. Very often we would find the cupboards had been emptied with all their contents neatly piled up on the worktop underneath.*

There may have been a little panic in his voice, but there was a touch of urgency when he stated, *'Just the other day a customer walked out with wet hair after witnessing a chair wheel itself from a workstation into the centre of the salon. She was the only one present in the room. Both my customers and staff members are beginning to leave. My business is falling apart. The entire experience has made me extremely uncomfortable and I try not to be alone in my own salon. I need you to come in as soon as possible as I'm becoming more than a little concerned.'*

Through word of mouth, stories were being told of the unnatural happenings occurring at the salon. A local paper gotten wind of the proceedings and contacted Ian asking if they could write a piece about the strange activity they were experiencing at the salon. He said, *'Word had already gotten out, so I thought what could I lose from allowing them to write about it.'* The article was entitled "A hair-raising experience." ITV also got in touch as they were airing a pilot TV programme on the paranormal happenings around locations within the East Anglian regions. They interviewed some of the staff, but Ian declined to be interviewed.

The conversation finished with Ian asking me how soon I could come and investigate the building saying he would like to accompany me.

It was a clear evening with a full moon for my visit to the salon. I parked my car in the square opposite, facing the building. On approaching the property, my attention was drawn to a small attic window where the face of a child was looking down at me. At first, I thought it to be the reflection of the moon. I'd stood for some time trying to see if it was male or female when the image suddenly disappeared. Ian was already inside the building and had left the door ajar waiting for me to join him. The reception lights were on, illuminating the entire downstairs. He greeted me and asked, *'What's the plan?'*

I informed him I like to walk around the property identifying any areas of high energy concentration. I also take note of areas with a negative vibration or possible portal activity developing an imprint of the location as such. Ian wasn't happy with this approach and felt we needed to get down to the heart of the matter. He was very insistent that he wanted me to go straight into connecting with any residual spirits that reside there. I was being asked to start a puzzle without having any pieces. This threw me a little. I like to gather knowledge of the premise to build a psychic profile of what is happening and what will role will be in resolving the matter. It also gives my guides time to advise me of any issues and dangers.

Ian asked, *'What causes hauntings? Why do they happen?'* I'd explained it could be many things, but what came to mind in Ian's current circumstances is quite common. When renovation work is being carried out, the noise vibration and general movement of the fabric of the property can disturb any residual energy. He confirmed, *'Thinking back, there did seem to be a connection when the renovation works began and to the heightened spirit activity.'*

Going through into the salon, I'd diminished the overhead light in preference for lighting a candle to heighten our senses. I'd placed a tape recorder between us in the hope of recording EVP. We sat quietly for some time in silence. I could feel we had been joined and had attracted the interest from many spirits. After a short time, we heard someone whistling, one long continuous blow. It seemed to come from the far end of the room. This was then followed moments later by another whistle, with a slightly different tone. Ian & I just looked at each other. Saying nothing, we gestured that we had both heard the same thing. It was after the whistle, I felt an intense energy was beginning to fill the room of a dark and sinister nature.

There was a series of other noises. They seemed to be coming from the reception area next door. We could hear heavy footsteps together with what sounded like a squeaky door opening and closing along with other general taps and bangs. After the noises stopped, we went on a hunt to track down where the noise might have come from. We opened and closed all doors to ascertain if any of these had been the one that caused that squeak that stood out to us. None of the doors were making any sounds, much less a squeak.

Moving over to the reception desk, we noticed the business cards had been placed in a precise manner and were laid side by side in a row. A biro pen was balancing precariously across the top of other pens and pencils that were stood in the pot. We rewound the recorder to see if we had captured anything and heard a series of different sounds. There was a pause where nothing was heard before a little girl spoke, with a slight accent *'Can you help me please?'* Ian jumped back; startled and was really shaken by her message.

Ian could also sense the heightening of energy was building and began to feel very uncomfortable with it and declared, he'd had enough for one night and was going home. He asked me to return as soon as I could to continue with the investigation.

I felt sure many lost souls were residing here. I'd also sensed that most were children and one, that wasn't a child, was a dark and disturbing energy. Ian informed me, whilst locking up the front door, that he would not be joining me on my next visit. This was a fascinating place, I couldn't wait to see what it had to reveal.

The following day, I called to rebook a suitable time for my return visit. The salon was abuzz with staff wanting to know what had happened. Ian had explained to them about the many strange noises and of the EVP recording of the young girl's voice. Some were scared, others inquisitive. Two staff members had asked if they could accompany me when I returned to the property. I thought this was a good idea as they were familiar with the building and of the many sounds the old building tends to generally make.

I had formed a group, some years previous, for people with a healthy interest in the paranormal. On occasions, I would invite them to accompany me on a case. Louise, a group member, was a talented psychic artist and Ann, a budding historian revelled in the joy of unearthing historical data. Both were a great asset to the group. Ann would take notes on any dates or names that may be given by any of the group during the investigation and then research the historical archives to validate the information that had come through. Louise would walk amongst us and when she felt a surge of energy, she would draw an impression that came into her mind. Often, she would include names and detail about the characters she drew. There were seven of us in total on the evening of the investigation, including the two members of staff.

As a group, we walked through the many rooms together with our minds open, tapping into the subtle energies from each of the areas we focused on. Almost all of us experienced a strong aroma of burning or smouldering wood as we walked up the second staircase, towards the attic rooms.

The small rooms at the top of the building had been adapted for beauty and therapy treatments and decorated in tones of delicate pastel creams and pinks. It was very calming visually with a pleasant aroma of lavender that greeted us as we entered. Although the visual aspects of this room were very pleasing, it held strong negative vibrations that gave me cause for alarm. As soon as Louise entered the room she felt strong impressions flooding her mind. Her pencil began moving across the paper with great speed. Some members had gathered around her to watch the image unfold.

My attention was drawn to a small wall. A cupboard in the corner of the room had gained my interest. As I opened the doors to the cupboard, a heavy feeling of oppression ran through me. Many in my group experienced the same vibration. I'd felt a strong sensation to my solar plexus akin to being physically struck. For me, this is a sign which resonates that great trauma has taken place. The historic energy had impressed itself within the fabric of the walls, leaving a residual trace. The emotion experienced by some of the group was so intense they were feeling overwhelmed and left the room. Ann, the historian, was asking out loud, *'any impressions please, names, dates?'*
The two members of staff were standing close together starring into the cupboard, pointing into its confines. Look they said, you can see the old staircase at the back of the cupboard. On closer examination, one could clearly see the back of the original stairs as they continued upwards until they ran into where they had been bricked off. Ann was excited about this part of the wing and remarked she would research as to why this was so.

As I went to close the cupboard, I saw a brief glimpse of two small spirit children huddled together. Their eyes were wide with fear. Their clothes were greyish in colour with each wearing an old worn out shirt with scruffy trousers. They both wore small ankle boots of which had seen better days. I initially jumped back as it wasn't something that I expected to see. They knew I could see them and I feel this frightened them even more. The younger boy aged around five years old was clinging tightly to the arm of the elder one. They resembled each other in their features and colouring. I assumed they must be brothers.

I gently spoke to them, keeping the door slightly ajar. *'Don't be afraid.'* I said, *'Do you need help?'* The elder boy spoke saying, *'We are afraid to leave. We're scared the master will find us.'* The sadness and fear that oozed from them was intense.

Just then, a stern male voice was heard by everyone in the room. It startled me and made me jump. The direct voice screeched, at close range to my ears, *'Get out!'* The two staff members were terrified and held onto each other for support. Turning my focus back to the cupboard, the boys had vanished. I tried several times to call them back, but sadly they did not return.

Louise turned the sketch pad around to reveal the portrait she had drawn. A man with cold motionless eyes and high protruding cheekbones looked back at me. His dark bushy sideburns ran down the length of his long jaw bone. Louise had signed off as, 'The Master.' She had not clairvoyantly heard the two boys in the cupboard mention his name. The overall impression of aggression was felt from this character. Louise shuddered when describing how he'd made her feel when drawing him. I knew his vibration was dark and very significant to the strange happenings experienced within this building.

Some of the group had already dispersed and entered the other beauty rooms located on the middle floor. A loud cry was heard from one of them. As I approached her, she held her arms outstretched revealing three deep scratches from her inner elbow to wrist. An EVP recording had captured a male's angry inaudible growl. I was informed she had been overzealous. She had been calling out, mocking the spirits. She was demanding they reveal themselves. She was naturally shaken by the experience and became a little less verbal for the rest of the investigation. I would personally not encourage tormenting any spirit, as you may experience more than you can handle. The entity will go to any lengths to sustain his control.

I don't think many people fully understand how a Rescue Medium works. How would they? When things of this nature happen, it's usually behind closed doors and never spoken of for fear of being alienated. It is almost as if people are afraid they might catch paranormal disease from you. It could also be the fear of what they don't understand that drives this behaviour of not wanting to know. It must be remembered we are dealing with people. Albeit, they are in spirit form. They are still driven by a desire and they feel they have their reasons for doing what they do. The only difference is that they no longer have a biological suit (a human body). They require the energy produced by others to remain in existence.

A few members and I were using a small table as a communication tool. Almost immediately, as soon as we placed our finger tips on the table, it began to move. We quickly established what would be a yes response and a no response. We asked several questions out loud. Ann had asked '*knock for how many spirits are resident here in this building.*' The answer we received came back with twelve consecutive knocks. She asked again, '*Is there spirit children present?*' Again, we received one loud knock for a yes response.

She continued questioning on behalf of the group '*Do you seek our help for release into the light?*' We heard a loud tap on the centre of the table and it began to move around the room at great speed. '*Is there a force preventing you from doing so?*' again another deep thud came in response.

I had asked Louise, to place the portrait onto the centre of the table. The table had stopped abruptly. Ann asked out loud *'Do you recognise this individual?'* One single loud tap, for yes, was given in response. Then suddenly, the picture was swiped off the table. We were receiving answers to our questions immediately. It was if they were trying to get as much information to us as they could before they would have to go.

We continued asking questions for a little while longer. Ann asked, *'Is he the one preventing your entry into the light?'* Again, one single tap for yes was given. *'Is he with you now?'* she asked. A few moments later we heard two distinctive taps for no. We could feel the energy had dropped and seemed to be depleting. We decided to discontinue using this method as no further information could be gathered from this basic form of communication. Ann had taken note of all the questions and answers of which we had asked. She was hoping this would aid her research into the property and its inhabitants.

It was now early morning. I was alone, checking that everyone had left the attic and middle floor rooms, as we were heading downstairs for a refreshment break, prior to conducting the séance and rescue. My guides had informed me the spirit children were all together in the same time frame. They had all passed around the same time and were all seeking release. The one they call 'The Master' seemed to have a hold over their souls.

On walking down, the stairs, I'd caught a glimpse of my reflection in the full-length mirror that overhung the lower staircase. I was surprised to see luminous green wispy lights swirling around my body. I was transfixed on the scene before me. These lights started to solidify and form into solid masses. Many faces, all of the children of varying ages, began pulsating in and out of focus. My guides had informed me that the green ectoplasm lights were the energy of the children, trying to gain my attention.

I was feeling uneasy so as a precaution, I mentally called in my guide, Zulu. I had only just re-enforced my protection when I suddenly began to experience a deep pressure to the middle of my back. A strong force was pushing me forwards down the stairs. I'd been momentarily taken off guard, giving him a prime opportunity to do as much damage to me as possible. I reached out to grab the handrails, either side of me, in order to steady myself as I was under physical psychic attack. 'The Master' was making his intentions clear. Luckily, I had grabbed the handrails just in time. He was demonstrating his dislike of having me present and this was a warning for me to back off. He was a malicious entity; whose intent is to cause harm if threatened and would do whatever he could to secure his dominance in this existence.

Though the children were afraid of the 'The Master,' they were showing their allegiance and support for me by revealing themselves in the green light during the 'The Master's' presence. They were too weak to be of any significance against the 'The Master,' yet they remained with me during the ordeal. Their presence is best described as children running to their mum's protection while she was being abused. They knew I was their path to freedom and I felt as if they were saying to me, *'You can't get hurt, you're our only way out.'*

Louise had just walked through from the kitchen to the reception area with a coffee cup in hand. She'd glanced up and noticed my strange contorted posture as I desperately hung on to the handrails of the staircase. I could see, within the mirror, my form was disjointed. The alinement of my spine was twisted to such a degree. *'Oh, my God!'* she called out, as she placed her cup down on the reception desk. *'You're surrounded by lights.'* Seeing my plight, she attempted to approach me. Louise only reached the third step. An unforeseen force physically lifted her in to the air, separating her feet from the floor. She was pushed backwards. Thankfully, she somehow landed onto the reception couch that was behind her.

I was desperately trying to move but couldn't. It's was as if I had been zapped by a stun gun delivering strong nerve sensations that ran up and down my spine. I could feel the sensation of a burning hot liquid travelling around my neck. Looking at my reflection in the mirror, I could see a raised, red, welt line appearing. I really wanted to take my hands off the rails to rub the affected area, but I knew if I did, I would lose my balance and fall down the stairs.

Louise had recovered. She looked up at me. Then she reached for her sketch book and started furiously sketching. '*Look!*' She said, as she pointed at me, '*Look at what's happening to you!*' I could clearly see in the mirror my features changing. I was transfiguring. My face had become long and drawn with high predominant cheekbones. Staring back at me, in the mirror, where these deep, dark-set eyes which held a look of hatred. My lips were thin, my nose was long and bearing a slight hook. 'The Master' was placing his features, like a mask, upon my own.

The others had come back into the reception area after hearing Louise's remarks. They were watching my transfiguration, while gathering together at the bottom of the stairs. 'The Master' was now trying to get into my head. He was having an effect on my thoughts, causing me to feel intense anger. I had great difficulty holding back the urge to want to spit on the group. Within my mind, I could hear 'The Master' screaming the words '*WHORES, THE LOT OF YOU ARE WHORES!*'

My mind came back into focus when I saw the white flashes from the cameras, as photos were being taken. I was distinctly aware of a sensation of my Zulu guide drawing close beside me. The pressure in my back began to ease. The green swirling mass of ectoplasm had disappeared, along with the faces. As my physique returned to normal, I felt safe to loosen my grip on the handrails. The photos taken held poor quality. Only one distorted image came out with blurred colours. With batteries drained, causing cameras to dis-function, there wasn't any photographic evidence of the battle that had occurred.

The telephone on the reception desk rang, startling us all. I'd noticed from the large clock, that hung on the reception wall, that it was 2.30am. One of the staff members picked up the phone. They thought it be Ian checking in to see how we were getting on. Her eyes held a frightening expression, as she listened to the call. She thrust the phone towards me, clearly shaking, reaching for the support from her work colleague. A male's angry tone growled down the phone. I'd pressed the loudspeaker so that everyone present could hear. I'd asked him what he wanted. The phone went dead. You could hear a pin drop. Everyone was fixed on the spot. I'd dialled to see what number was registered as the last caller. The call hadn't registered and referred to a call received the previous day.

Suddenly, the chip and Pin credit card device came alive. It began spitting out blank paper roll. The staff jumped back in alarm. They remarked, *'This has never happened before.'* The device carried on for some time until reaching the end of the roll. The paper had spilt out, covering the counter.

Several of the team had jumped when a loud noise came from the salon. We all ran out to see what had caused it and saw what was a tall pyramid display of used hair products had been knocked down. Tins were scattered everywhere, some were still rolling across the floor heading in different directions.

I felt now was the time to get the group to form a circle. I placed a tape recorder in the centre. While I was bent down, I became aware of a pair of eyes watching me from the corner of the room. The shadowy image of a young boy was materialising. He looked as if he was soaked through to the skin. His dark lank hair and his emaciated frame was a pitiful sight. Everyone present had also witnessed the dark shadow and vibrational change. I struck up communication with him through mental mediumship and asked him why he was so wet? I had a feeling I would have to be very gentle in my approach with him.

'I'm Jon,' he said, speaking with a cockney accent. *'Can yew elp us? We all needya elp, an Caffrine too.'* (Translation: Can you help us? We all need your help, and Catherine too).

Jon, confirmed how he had passed, telling me, *'a horse had kicked me in the head.'*

I asked, *'Was that your job? ... Looking after the horses?'*
He nodded yes.
I wanted to know more about the children, *'Are there many spirit children here?'*
'Yeh' Jon responded, *'loads.'*
'Do you know the one who calls himself "The Master?"' I said.
Jon looked downwards and shuffled slightly, looking uncomfortable before replying *'yeh, e as us trapped ere.'* (Translation: Yes, he has us trapped her.)

The group had formed a tight circle standing close to one another. I called my clearance guides to surround us with a protective shield of light. Louise, the psychic artist had positioned herself in the centre of the circle. Her full concentration upon her pencil, as it drew an image that seemed to come alive. She remarked, *'I feel the spirit of a young girl is with me.'* The image of a small child, with long flowing hair and elf like features, transformed from the paper. The group were all observing the awakening of the sketch as it was drawn. Louise had signed it Catherine. She had no prior knowledge of the name, as Jon had given it to me through our mental mediumship connection. At this stage, I had not shared this part of the information with the group.

The lighting in the room was dim apart from a small flickering candle that stood in the centre of our circle. We all stood very quietly. We were all experiencing the room temperature drop. Louise's drawing of Catherine revealed a little girl wearing a pinafore dress, with a petticoat that showed just below the hemline and ankle height, lace-up boots.

The sketch of Catherine highlighted, within the flickering candlelight, was the group's focus of attention. I'd reinforced grounding and protection techniques as I always do, just prior to a release. Only moments had passed when the sound of soft shuffling footsteps and whispering voices were heard. Something, still yet unseen, was approaching us from behind. A single whistle blow was heard, then another, with a slightly different tone, as if in reply. This was the same as what Ian and myself had heard our first night. I'd felt this was a method of communication the children had used for each other.

We watched mesmerised, how the flickering of the candle reacted when its elongated flame lent from one side to the other as if a gentle breeze was affecting it. No one was moving and there were no draughts. Jon stood back hesitating, just outside our circle. I spoke out loud for him to come forward and noticed that many spirit children had joined him. I asked him to bring them forward.

One by one, each of the group members had remarked they had experienced being touched. I'd asked them to remain calm and not to break the circle under any circumstances. Each spirit child stood beside a member of the group. Some had placed their hands on a member's hand. Others had touched them on the shoulder or arm. I could not see Catherine amongst them. My eyes scanned the room for Jon. He was no longer present.

The gentle sound of a high-pitched tinkling bell was heard by us all. A moment later, it fell silent. The air was charged with electricity. I caught sight of Jon, who was walking beside Catherine as if giving her support to approach the circle and enter its centre.

Each one of the spirit children had gathered around them. Catherine held something in her hand. It was held loosely by her side of which dangled down towards her knees. She looked shy and nervous, but constantly looked to Jon for reassurance. It was a strange scene unfolding before us. Children were materialising in front of us. There was a variety of ages and different heights. They were transforming, becoming almost solid in form. Some were clearer to see than others. Catherine's hologram-like image was becoming clearer. It was now possible to see what she held in her hands. She was holding a teddy bear by its arm.

The group fell silent, taking in the vision before them. Not one dared to even swallow should they alter the vibration. The temperature dropping dramatically, so much so, some of the group had begun to shiver. The candle flame had reached such a height that it seemed impossible to achieve, resembling a thin white line. The electric energy within the room was growing stronger, stimulating the hairs on my arms to rise. A strong feeling of anticipation was felt by all. The vibration felt as if it was charging in readiness for angelic beings to come forth and release these children from this hell.

Just as we thought we were going to see the children released, we were startled out of our silence by loud bangs that seemed to come from beneath us. The force was great, the floor was vibrating underfoot. The group, working as one energy, began reciting a prayer out loud. We chanted repeatedly with a crescendo of voices. The sound resonance within the room was powerful. The banging intensified as if trying to drown out our voices. Objects started flying off the shelves. A salon chair, on wheels, was pushed with great force from the other side of the room towards us in an attempt to break up the circle. The presence of 'The Master' had joined us. He was doing everything he could to distract our attention. The group was determined and remained firm. Our hands were still linked as we moved in slightly closer, enclosing the circle further. We were creating a protective wall to surround the children from his control. We did not want him to enter the centre and stop the cleanse. We needed to keep him separated from the children.

The entire room began to fill with a golden glow of light. It was as if sunlight was streaming through with its powerful rays. The vibrational energy lifted and was now feeling very different. All the noise and distractions with the room falling silent. None of us moved or said a word. We just marvelled at the transformation within the room. It was an extremely emotional experience for us all. I'd noticed the expressions on the children's faces change. They seemed to lose the furrows of anxiety and pain. Their eyes became animated and happy.

I could feel how privileged we were to be witnessing this angelic spectacle. The light was surrounding our circle as we stood around the children. We felt so safe. The children started to link hands with each other. This beautiful vibrant light had begun to slowly intensify, making it difficult to see. It was similar to when the sun comes through your car window and you can't see a thing. Very slowly, the light began to fade as did the image of the children with each child slowly becoming translucent till we could no longer see them. We knew they were being rescued by the Angelic realm. You could see the happiness in their faces as they embraced their transition into the light.

The warmth was ebbing back into the room once more. The room was calm with the only sound being a gentle tinkling, followed by a slight thud. An object was lying on the floor within the circle. It was a tiny golden bell attached to a red ribbon. It was the one that was placed around the collar of Catherine's teddy bear. I wondered if this was her way of letting us know she had gone.

We all agreed to meet up in a couple of weeks after the investigation for a conclusion of all that was brought through. Enough time for Ann, the historian, to gather historical facts and to validate any dates or names that were given during the investigation. We had given Ian a written report along with the psychic artist drawings of Catherine and 'The Master.'

Summary:
It was interesting to note that Ann had found from recorded archives that in 1835 a Union workhouse was erected near to where Hendricks stood. It was to accommodate 300 inmates made up of mainly orphaned children. This Grade 11 building was once used as a china factory.

The one they referred to as 'The Master' was in charge, having many of the workhouse children to work for him. The children would have come from many different regions and would account for the different accents heard.

Ann had taken notes from the group when they identified the smell of burning on the second staircase towards the attic. She found a historical record that mentioned a fire which had damaged the whole wing of the property. She also found a list of children's names from the workhouse, Jon and Catherine were amongst them. We believe the two brothers, who were huddled together in the top cupboard, had perished in the fire, as did many others.

Ann revealed that the owner was found hanging by his neck in the hallway, above the stairs. It was said he was perverted and bore the blame for the fire outbreak. It was the same area where he had psychically attacked me.

The backyard, where young Jon had lost his life, was once the stable area which had housed the horse & cart for transporting the china. The large metal pully hook is still very much in place situated above the arch, where the cart would have stood, lowering the crates of pottery.

There was no further mention of spirit children being heard or seen. Some years later, the property changed hands again. It now has a different business operating from within its walls.

Chapter 4

Fear of Redemption

It was a lovely day in Bedfordshire. Jade was enjoying the view out of her rear garden window. She was watching her children playing outside. They were enjoying themselves without a care in the world as children do when using their imagination in play. Then, without warning, the scene changed. Initially, Jade had to refocus her eyes as she couldn't believe what she was seeing. She froze in fear as she saw her children being picked up into the air. There was no one there! Her children had just been swooped up and were levitating a few feet off the ground. Then, before she could move and to her horror, her children were suddenly thrust back down to earth face forward as if someone had thrown them down. Luckily, the children were only shaken and upset. Neither child was hurt. It was after this incident that I received a call for help.

Jade and her husband are a 30 something couple with two young children, a daughter and a son. Their house is a 70's style home located on a housing estate that fits in nicely with the surrounding houses. Before Jade and her husband purchased the property, it had been unoccupied for quite some time.

Even from Jade's first visit to the house, she felt something was off as she entered the property and experienced a cold shudder that ran down the middle of her spine. She thought the eerie vibration was from the bold white imprints that remained from where crucifixes had once been hung above each of the doorways. Once they moved in, she found out it was far worse. After only being moved in for a few weeks, they started experiencing unnatural and frightening activity in their home. Each child had their own room. Of a night, one of the children would wake up frightened and scream for their parents. They would say there was a man in their room looking at them. When the children were asked to explain further, they said he would stand at the foot of their bed and stare at them. This, of course had frightened the children greatly.

Word had started to spread about the unnatural activity occurring in the home. As mediums and paranormal groups learned of the encounters, they were soon knocking at the door for their chance to capture and record the strange happenings. Many only thought this to be simple poltergeist activity and were amused as the spirit would put on a show as if playing to an audience. Lights would turn on and off and strange light anomalies were caught on cameras and video equipment.

Things were starting to get too much for Jade. She was being bombarded by sensitives wanting to investigate her property, yet none of them seemed to take notice of her plight and the need to remove the spirit. Their visits did nothing to help ease her fears and worries. They only seemed to heighten the activity in the house and raise the intensity. Adding to this were daily calls from a social media site wanting to hear all the facts about the day's activities as if this was some sort of reality program.

Jade was under great pressure and fear. She felt her only hope was to ask a local priest to come in and perform a blessing. She was not particularly religious but had felt she had nowhere else to turn. She accompanied the priest as he went through the house sprinkling holy water and reciting Latin quotes in each of the rooms. Their home was quiet with no activity for several days after. She hoped her nightmare was at an end, but unfortunately, that wasn't the case and the incidents soon returned.

During my initial telephone conversation with Jade, my guides informed me that both the children were the focus of the spirit's attention. They were at risk of being physically harmed and more. Vampires draw energy from their victims which allows them supernatural healing and longevity. In this case, the visitor was drawing energy from the children, much like a vampire, to maintain his existence. Without this energy, he wouldn't be able to remain connected to the earth plane. The syphoning of the children's energy would undoubtedly lead to impaired health issues if it hadn't already. I put the question to Jade about her children's health. She confirmed that both her children had been diagnosed with an autoimmune deficiency and that doctors could not find the reason. Numerous tests were being carried out, but nothing had been identified as to the cause of their lethargy and sickness.

This was definitely a case that needed to be sorted as a matter of urgency. The longer the children were exposed to this danger, the more harm that could take place in one fashion or another. Luckily, our dates matched up and I would be able to see her within the week. I asked that her husband and children weren't present during the meeting. They would need to stay somewhere away from the property during my investigation. Her husband arranged for them to go over to his parents' home on the day of the cleanse and they would stay the night, just to be on the safe side. Jade's sister would come over that morning to keep her company and provide moral support during the cleanse.

The day of the cleanse was upon us. Knowing that the spirit in the house was of a negative disposition, I asked for permission from Jade for my paranormal group to accompany me. I wanted to give them the chance to experience how a negative energy feels. We arrived as a group. I sat in my car for a moment going over my notes that I had taken from my guides after our phone call. I was being directed to concentrate on the children's bedrooms. It was also imperative to find the portal that the spirit was using to access the home. A portal is like a wormhole of energy. It allows a spirit to travel from one dimension into another. In this case, it was being used to enter our dimension and more specifically Jade's home. Portals are often associated with cold drafts and strong vibrations.

Jade came out of her house and walked over to me while I was still sitting in my car. She had left the front door open and I could see her sister was in the hallway sweeping the floor. Jade seemed rattled and was very keen to get me inside. Walking through the doorway, I was told to watch where I stood as there was glass everywhere.

Jade, in an excited voice, began to explain, *'We (Jade and her sister) were sitting in the kitchen having a cup of coffee waiting for you to arrive. The kitchen door was open to view the hallway and the front door. We noticed the temperature in the kitchen had suddenly dropped. We then both turned to each other and commented that we felt as if we were being watched.'* Jade described that she heard a sound coming from the long narrow hallway. They both jumped up, standing close to each other for support and together, they hesitantly went to investigate what could be the cause. As they crossed the threshold into the hallway, they could smell an unpleasant aroma. Jade said, *'It was awful.'* It seemed to be emanating from upstairs and coming down the staircase. The odour got worse and became more pungent. Then, whispering voices started. It wasn't anything they could understand, and it wasn't being spoken from any particular direction making it somewhat disorientating.

Walking gingerly, almost creeping, towards the front door, they stopped in their tracks standing motionless. Halfway down the hallway, they could see the large ornate mirror slowly rise up the wall. Jade continued, *'It disconnected itself from the hooks* (that held it in place).' It moved upwards, towards ceiling height. Still rooted to the spot in fear, with their eyes transfixed, the mirror began moving eerily towards them. It kept perfect contact with the wall and then the ceiling. It slowly crept along the ceiling until it got just above their heads. Then, it suddenly broke free. It came down with an almighty crash. The mirror narrowly missed the sisters and shattered on the wooden floor. As Jade bent down to pick up one of the larger shards, she said, *'I saw a man's eyes staring directly at me. They were so intense.* You could see from her expression and mannerisms that this had shaken her. She had gotten a glimpse of the spirit that had been making her life a nightmare. The spirit was clearly demonstrating his anger as he knew my purpose at the home. He wasn't going to try and entertain me with a light display of flicking light switches on and off. He was sending me a warning that he intended to stay.

Jade told me, *'That isn't the only thing that has happened. Last night, all hell had broken out!'* It is often the case, that just prior to my visit, the spirit visitor will increase paranormal activity as if disapproving of my visit. She explained, *'At 3:12 am, my husband and I were woken up by a loud scratching and banging sound that was coming from the attic. We sat perfectly still in our bed. We didn't dare breathe. We just listened. The sound was similar to a heavy object being dragged,* they were both now wide awake and looking at each other wondering what the hell. She continued, *'When suddenly, with force, the attic hatch door flipped wide open, scaring us half to death! We sat straight up in our bed as this thing jumped down through the attic into the hallway.'* Both were certain it was male as it was almost solid in appearance.

'We were extremely frightened, almost paralysed with fear. That's when we heard a loud growling sound come from it.' said Jade. With great speed, it had taken off into their daughter's bedroom. Their daughter woke up startled and began to scream. They jumped out of their bed and rescued their daughter from the room. Their son at this stage was not being affected and had remained asleep. The rest of the night went without incident.

I told Jade I would like a tour of the house so that I could see if I can pick up any unnatural vibrations or negative signatures. As we walked throughout the house, I was able to identify where areas of highly charged energy had gathered. We made our way to the daughter's bedroom. The atmosphere was very heavy. It held a dark and suffocating energy and was extremely different from the rest of the house. Jade confirmed that this room was the height of spirit activity and that the dogs wouldn't even enter this room. Jade remarked that *'the tv in here has never worked properly. It turns itself on and off. Yet, when we put it in another room, it works fine.'* Her daughter never wanted to spend any time in the bedroom, much less go to bed. Jade talked of the terrible unaccountable smells that would just appear and that no deodorisers could get rid of it. They even redecorated the room with delicate colours and laid a new carpet but nothing could convince their daughter to want to stay in the room.

As I walked out of the daughter's bedroom, the hairs on my arms and neck had stood up on end. Something was behind me and I felt an intense surge of negative energy surround me. It initially took me off-guard. A mass of dark ectoplasmic energy began to materialise in the corner of the bedroom. I moved towards it with my eyes focused on the image. A male figure was slowly starting to form. I distinctly saw his attire and a dog collar around his neck identifying him as a reverend. Jade had confirmed a clergyman had lived in the home previously as neighbours had told her and the fact that she still occasionally receives post for him at this address.

Face to face, I directed my thoughts into contacting him clairvoyantly in hopes to communicate with him. What did this troubled spirit want? I sensed his vibration as very agitated. He was screaming at me, in my mind through telepathy. No one else could hear what he was saying or at the intensity in which he was saying it. *'IT'S MY LETTER! IT'S MY BOOK! I WANT THEM.'* He said in a heightened and aggressive manner. He was trying to be stern with me, demanding that he wanted his book and letters. Speaking aloud so that everyone could hear, I repeated what I had been asked. Jade divulged that mail had arrived the other day for the clergyman and that a letter was in her car to return to sender. I asked her to get the letter for me; of which she did.

Jade came back with the letter and handed it to me. The postmark was from India. The contents were from other reverends and religious factions working at a children's sanctuary. The Spirit Reverend was extremely agitated over something as simple as a letter. I wanted to know why this letter was so important to him. What difference could a letter make to someone on the other side? His intensity of asking for something materialistic could serve no purpose. I wanted to know what this letter was about.

With the letter in hand, I stuck my finger into the crease of the envelope and ripped the letter open. He was livid. An anger was sparked in him so great, that the whole room was blackened and had become like a vortex of energy.
He was furious and lashed out. He grabbed at my arm causing me physical pain, like that of a Chinese burn. I

held out my arm so that they could all witness the fingertip bruising starting to appear.

Jade complained of feeling dizzy and nauseous. The aroma in the room had become vile. Bad drains would not suffice to identify the smell. I'd asked out loud for protection for us all and started to pray for the soul of the Spirit Reverend. Even though he was a man of the cloth, he didn't seem to appreciate my prayers.

He was desperate to rile me and was trying to intimidate me with breathing his cold stank breath across my face.

His bellowing voice screamed for all to hear (and was captured on my voice recorder). His words, *'I am the voice and I say you MOVE!'*

He was trying to threaten me with his dominance in the hope I would retreat. I was having none of it. I was standing my ground, showing defiance. He could see my strength for if I showed any sign of weakness, he would be able to use it against me and potentially the group. It could also threaten him being successfully evicted from the home.

Praying even louder, I glanced over towards Jade. She had gone completely white; her face had drained of all colour. *'JADE!'* I shouted trying to get her attention. She turned her face in my direction but held a glazed look. Dark circles appeared and surrounded both her eyes. She was staring at me, but I could see she was not focusing. I knew he was affecting her. I reached forward and grabbed her hands as she was raised upwards off the floor levitating a few inches in the air.

Jade's sister was frantic in the background amongst all the commotion. I had somehow managed to get Jade back and focusing on me. The back of her head had begun to involuntarily hit the wall with violent thuds. She was silent and held a transfixed expression on her face. Her terrified eyes linked to mine as if pleading for me to get him to stop. Her sister was terrified as she witnessed this assault. I spoke aloud demanding that he release her immediately, 'RELEASE HER! RELEASE HER NOW!' and within a few seconds, he did.

Through mental mediumship, his focus had changed from the letter to his book. He demanded that I give him his book. I relayed to the group what I was hearing in my mind. Jade was recovering from her shock and was being comforted by her sister. I could concentrate more on the Spirit Reverend now that the two sisters were out of the way. He repeated to me, 'I want my book!' I had received a mental download to leave the bedroom and go into the boy's bedroom. I still didn't have the full picture, but the message from guides was one of urgency that I must go into that room. I stormed out of the daughter's room and into the son's bedroom with Jade's sister following in hot pursuit.

Entering the room, I could see the Spirit Reverend's image so clearly. He looked like a stern, no-nonsense character with very thin lips. His facial features were sharp with high cheekbones and a pointed nose. He was balding with receding white hair that was brushed back. For a clergyman, he had a very apathetic vibration about him.

I walked past him as if he wasn't there and stood beside the tall fitted built-in wardrobe. My guides sent me a vision of myself pointing to the highest cupboard. I knew they wanted me to look in there. Jade had joined me in the room. She commented, 'There's nothing in there. It's only my son's action men and Lego bricks.' The Spirit Reverend stood to the side of the wardrobe watching my every move. He was now quite insistent that his book was in the wardrobe and I knew where. One of the group brought me a chair so that I could reach the top shelf. I could feel his anxiety building. He was talking so fast in my mind with Jade interjecting, *There was nothing left in the house prior to us moving in. The house was empty.'* I said openly, *'His saying the book is up there, and that he wants it.'*

As I reached deep into the wardrobe, a very large, white, ornate bible was found. It was so heavy that it needed two hands to hold it. A bookmark had been placed in the book at a passage marked "come unto thee, little children." The bookmark was their daughter's latest school photo, taken only a month previously. They had not seen that photo for some time, much less known about the existence of the Bible in their son's bedroom. The Bible was over 1ft in size and very heavy. I couldn't help but ask myself how something that large could have spiritually materialized. Then there was the question of why did he have the school photograph of their daughter as a bookmark, highlighting a children's passage.

I opened the Bible to the bookmarked passage and read it out loud. Still holding the letter in my hands, I began to tear it up. As I did so, I raised my voice asking why he was angry and why he refused to enter into the light. His answer through mental mediumship was shocking as he revealed he was frightened of redemption. He was guilty of wrongdoings to children. He knew he would need to have to face the consequences for his actions. He'd been hiding behind the security and camouflage of his dog collar for many years, allowing him safe passage for his paedophile addiction. He knew this was wrong and that judgment day was beckoning. He preferred to stay in the grey matter, the in-between realms, rather than face the consequences of his sins.

The penny had dropped who he was, what he was doing and what his intentions were. The letter, along with what we had already learned, showed he was involved with other religious fractions connected to orphanages. As my role as a spiritual communicator, I try and act for both sides in trying to find a solution to the problem but by his actions, I could not allow this to continue. There was nothing he could say that would make me listen. I was done, and it was time for him to meet his maker. I asked my guides to collect him, for him to start his journey for forgiveness and to move on and leave this family in peace.

Some moments had passed. I had sensed a reluctance from him at first, caused by his own fears and then a release. I knew he had surrendered to what fate he must now face. It was done. I knew the higher beings had come and assisted him into the light. I have no part in this portion of the cleanse. I act merely as a power battery providing the energy enabling this to take place. My guides had informed me that the portal was in the attic. With the assistance of my guides, we shut down the portal to stop any other unwanted spirits coming through.

A healing prayer was given to Jade and the home was blessed. It was immediately noticed by all that the foul aroma had gone; the room had warmed and all had felt quiet and peaceful. Jade was instructed on how to use protective measures and mind energy techniques. The Bible was destroyed by burning each page on my log fire once back at my home.

Summary:
I received an update from Jade a few days later saying that they have not experienced any paranormal activity since my visit. She told me that they are all sleeping through the night and the health of both her son and daughter are

improving. They no longer require any further medical tests. The daughter is now happy to be in her room.

One question that remains outstanding is, why did the Reverend show his hand, figuratively speaking, picking up the children and dropping them? For, if he hadn't done this, the physical abuse wouldn't have been apparent to the parents resulting in the call to me. It would have probably just been treated as a haunting.

Chapter 5
The Malevolent Spirit

It was after having a brief conversation over the phone with a young woman, who was called Jenny. She had informed me she was concerned about her change of behaviour. She stated that her family and friends did not recognise her anymore, which lead them to feel uneasy in her presence. Unable to know what to suggest next, her parents became very distressed and had come to the conclusion that she was deranged. The conversation lead to her informing me that she had been seeing a psychiatrist for anger management. The weekly appointments did not make things any easier. I had interjected before she could reveal anymore as I had felt she had made an incorrect call to me. There was a brief silence. In an anxious voice she said, *'I'm experiencing some really weird stuff and I'm frightened of what I may do next…'*

A few days later we met up at my home for a consultation. Jenny asked if it was ok for her boyfriend to accompany her, as she wasn't currently driving. As they walked up the drive, through the drizzling rain, I noticed her boyfriend was gently leading her holding her by the hand. She had a petite frame, which became emphasised by her boyfriend's towering stature. She was very fortunate to have been blessed with Pixi like features, which made her appearance appear younger than she probably was. Her boyfriend, Shaun, looked to be of Indian descent. He seemed very relaxed in his demeanour.

I welcomed them into my home and asked them to go

through to the dining room. I noticed Jenny was nervous. Her body posture was tense and anxious. I was hoping that the dining room, with its invitingly warm and cosy atmosphere, would soon help her relax. I asked them to have a seat at the dining table whilst I made them a cup of tea. Jenny had taken the predominant seat positioned at the head of the large table whilst Shaun sat in the seat opposite to mine. I had felt this to be an unusual choice.

With her hands clasped in her lap, I knew the positioning of her seat would allow me to get a better read of her body language. I normally wouldn't have seen her hands if she had sat in the chair opposite to me. I'd wanted her to feel at ease and to relax as best she could. I felt this was going to be a difficult story for her to tell. *'You briefly told me over the phone you have been experiencing some weird stuff but didn't go into any details, how do you feel I may be of help?'*
Jenny glanced over to Shaun, who hadn't really spoken up to now, as this was his part to tell. Shaun explained, *'I suggested she attend one to of my religious healing circles Jenny seemed open to giving it a go but had felt uncomfortable whilst at the event. Afterwards, we ran into a relative of mine. I'd mentioned to him that Jenny needed some healing. My relative, of Seek religion, had previously come to you for a reading and knew of your other work including spirit rescue and felt she required this kind of help.'* After this, Shaun went back to his supporting role and didn't speak again until he was addressed.

I wanted to pick up on something that was stated during the phone conversation and asked her, *'You mentioned you had a fear. Can you tell me about what?'* She disclosed, *'I felt I was out of control and that my mind held dark thoughts.'* She'd believed herself to be evil.

Jenny went on to tell me her friends and family no longer recognised her. They said she displayed violent outbursts and had become very unpredictable in her actions. One by one, they had disassociated themselves from her. This left her very much isolated and in a depressed state of mind.

I was already aware of some of the details of Jenny's problem. My guides had started feeding me details related to her situation prior to our meeting. During the course of our conversation, I look for validation of what I have been told by my guides to confirm my interpretation and add it to the larger picture of what I'm seeing. Basically, I'm building a profile and looking for anomalies that give a clue as to what is going on. As a psychic profiler, I needed her to show me her hidden cards. I had a strong feeling she would hide behind a masquerade mask. This was already starting to reveal itself as a cat and mouse game. Patience was required and would pay great dividends.

Jenny, I'm not a counsellor and I don't intend going down that route with you.' I had said. *'That's not what I do. Saying that I still need to understand your past. Please take me back in time when you felt you had begun to feel different.'*

Jenny started to explain her story, *'It was around five years previous when things dramatically took a change for the worse.'* She seemed to look uncomfortable as she delved deeper into conversation revealing more of her background and of her daily life. She continued, *'I come from a fanatic Christian family where worship and our belief structure are very strong. This was why it had been a difficult decision in asking for help from another source. I feel our church has not been very helpful. Of course, my parents wouldn't talk about such nonsense'*

Her family prayed daily for her to be well and wholesome. They were at their wit's end. She continued, *'They felt I was presenting tendencies of having two distinct personalities. As a last resort, they made an appointment for me to see my GP for tests, upon where I was diagnosed as having schizophrenia.'*

As Jenny was speaking, I could see she was becoming more at ease and looking more comfortable with her surroundings. She created a very precise picture of how life was for her growing up. Being in a religious household, she had begun to feel oppressed with their righteousness.

'I used to be fun loving and so full of energy. I was working as an artist and had a large social network. I have no one now, only Shaun. Goodness knows why he puts up with me?' Jenny said as if asking for more sympathy from Shaun.

I asked, *'What's happening around you? Have any other members of the family felt or experienced anything un-towards?'* I wanted to identify if this was a schizophrenic or a paranormal episode. Both seem parallel in form.

Jenny replied, *'Umm, electrical items were the first dysfunctional things to happen. Light bulbs and battery-operated items just refused to work. At first, my Mum thought it was due to faulty wiring and shoddy building works, as the house we lived in was a new build and erected within a short period of time. We had lived there for several years. The house always seemed cold and Mum became miserable trying frantically to warm the place up. This frustrated her immensely to the point she decided it was time to move. She was getting neurotic and felt she was being watched all the time.'*

Trying to establish a time frame, I asked, *'Was this previous to the five years before things got bad?'*

'Yes.' Jenny continued, *'In the new home, we experienced no activity at all during the first year or so. This was to be short-lived. Paranormal type activity started with all things electrical especially when I went near to them. It was noticeable that my energy seemed to make matters worse.'*

I'm a twin to my sister and we have always been close but lately, we argue all the time. She's also experienced seeing some strange things but seems to be able to shrug them off. She's a different character entirely, to me. I've always envied her confidence and strength.' Jenny said, gently shuffling in the chair. The relationship with her sister obviously scratching a nerve.

I continued on this line with her, *'What did she experience?'* Jenny revealed, *'She would come into my bedroom. We would sit at the end of my bed having a chat. Then something weird would happen. We'd both see it.'*

Her story was jumping around. I questioned, *'Was this in your recent family home?'*
Jenny revealed, *'No. In the new build, strange random aromas would suddenly appear, such as cigarette smoke and lavender. On another occasion, we saw what looked like a black mist appearing in the corner of the room. The whole bedroom took on a very different atmosphere. I remember feeling quite upset and shaken by the whole experience. We both saw an outline shadow of a person silhouetted upon the wall. It had moved with great speed. I hunched myself up against my bedroom wall, covering myself with my quilt as the temperature had suddenly dropped. Jayne had briefly glanced over at me but said nothing. She didn't even react. I gave her a look that I knew she saw it. She shouted at me saying that she didn't see anything and that I was overreacting. She'd then stormed out of the room. It was after seeing the silhouette that bad luck seemed to encounter all who came in contact with me.'*

Again, I had to ask for a time check, *'So just to be clear, we aren't even at the five-year turn. You and your family are already experiencing 'weird stuff.'* Jenny replied, *'Yes.'*

At this stage, I didn't want to suggest anything paranormal was happening or otherwise. I was still questioning about schizophrenia vs paranormal. I had to keep an open mind. It has to be in her words. I wanted to know more about her family relationship and the role that played to where we are today. *'How do you feel about your family?'* I asked.

'I love them. I do. But I have no patience with them. I'm aware I'm getting worse.' I could see the frustration through micro-expressions on her face while she tried to keep control. I could also feel her anger starting to boil. *'I hear what's coming out of my mouth and at the same time, I have no control over it. Raising my voice in outbursts of anger, swearing and such like, are becoming the norm. My family take the burden of most of my stress upon themselves. This lead to them setting up my appointment with the GP where I was diagnosed. He then advised that I should have weekly counselling sessions to help with my anger issues. You could say I am overprotected to a degree. Reluctantly, I agreed to the weekly sessions along with my mum accompanying me. It wasn't easy for her. She wanted religious intervention. I was struggling with that side but kept quiet as I just wanted my own space.'*

I interjected, *'Was this when they got you your new home?'*

'Yes. I told them I wanted to live by myself and to have my own space. I was fortunate enough to have the finances provided by my Father. He purchased a small property, on my behalf, but I insisted it was to be in my sole name. I'd felt I was doing well and holding things together, or so I thought.' Jenny stated with her eyes giving a slight roll.

At this point, I was feeling something wasn't right. Things didn't seem to be adding up. During the original phone call with Jenny, I'd had a moment where I had tuned into her voice vibration and had felt an anger that was very different to what she was revealing. This followed with a telepathic download from my guides, after the call had ended, where information had begun to seep through automatically into my sub-conscious. I began jotting down the segments of information as they came into my mind, letting my intuition guide my pen onto the notepad. It was these notes I kept referring to as I felt this mismatch in vibrational energy.

I received an impression within my mind of a man who looked to be around 30-40 years of age. His hair was shorn close to his head with eyes that held a penetrating stare. His general appearance looked dishevelled. The most substantial sensation I received was his overwhelming energy of being menacing. I didn't at this stage know of whom I was receiving an impression of. The puzzle pieces were adding up and building a picture of which I couldn't ignore.

I had scribbled a rough sketch of what I'd felt to be a tattoo. I had seen it imprinted on the top of a man's hand. It ran close to the side of his thumb. The long blade of a dagger showed a serpent twisting around its entire length. This image was very precise. I knew it would be significant, but I wasn't sure how it would reveal itself. I did feel that now was not the time to divulge any of this to her.

Jenny had cut into my thoughts when she said, *'It was great having my own space but after a while, I'd begun to feel really lonely. I'd realised just how many friends I had lost contact with. My confidence was at an all-time low.'*

I took her back to the weekly sessions, *'Did you have a plan and were you feeling settled into your weekly sessions?'*
She explained, *'I was not familiar with the location of my new home. I had begun to walk around my new environment at night. This is when I felt most comfortable to go out. I often found myself just sitting on the bench in the local park. On my walks, I saw a group of men that had obviously fallen on hard times. Some were wrapped in blankets and most carried an assortment of carrier bags. I assumed must have held their only belongings. Strangely. I felt fascinated with this group. I was intrigued to know more about them. I wanted to talk to them and find out their individual stories.'*

'One had approached me and asked if I was ok? We struck up a conversation. The others, one by one had started to drift over to me. It was strange that I didn't feel intimidated by any of them. If anything, I felt a sense of belonging. I began seeing them regularly and knew of

the times they would generally meet up. I thought of them as my new friends. I would pop into Costa coffee and bring them hot drinks with muffins. They seemed to really appreciate this and welcomed me into their fold. I felt I was accepted as one of them after knowing them only a short time.'

'They introduced me to different things in my life I have never been exposed to. I so wanted to experiment with the things they were involved in and in no time at all, I'd experienced the effects of taking social drugs and intoxication from alcohol. I felt totally at home with my new-found friends. They were more than happy to share their substances with me, whether it was food, alcohol or drugs. I started buying fish n chips and a few cans of beer. We would sit around and all to eat together. I had found the happiness I had been searching for. I felt part of their family who accepted me for me.'

I could see where this was going. I made sure not to show any signs of my disapproval and asked, *"Did your parents know of this?'*

Jenny almost laughed but kept her composure. She said, *'No. I became a recluse. I was neglecting myself and others. I'd wear my day clothes for bed. I wouldn't even bother to shower. The only time I paid attention to my attire was when I attended my weekly therapy sessions. My counsellor advised my mother that she felt it would be wise for me to have further tests. She felt there was something they had missed in the diagnosis. I begrudgingly agreed and had the additional tests done. They diagnosed me with a form of psychosis and labelled me as a manic depressive. We carried on for some time with my weekly sessions, but I felt things were getting worse, not better.'*

Jenny continued, *'I had formed a bond with one of the group called Michael. He would obtain the drugs for me to which I became addicted.'*

Finally, Michael, the name I was waiting for. As much as I wanted to find out more about Michael, the time frames still weren't adding up. *'Just to make sure I have my time frames correct, we still aren't at the 5-year mark where the real changes started to occur?'*

Jenny said, *'That's correct. The winter was approaching fast and temperatures most evenings were dropping below zero. It felt wrong that I was laying in my warm bed and my friends were out there lying in shop doorways. They probably couldn't get into a shelter for the night.'*

'One cold frosty evening, I walked out onto the streets in search of them. I knew where they would most likely to be. There was one place, in particular, they liked to frequent. As expected, they were all sat together, huddled up in their many clothes and an array of cardboard packaging. I'd asked them all to come back to my home where it was warm and dry. They didn't hang around and followed me back home. In time, for the evenings only, it became their home too.'

'My family didn't visit me, as I was such a bad host. They had telephoned me daily, so there was little chance of them ever finding out.'

I appreciated Jenny now felt comfortable enough to reveal such personal details. I did wonder why she did not see the fact that the obsession with her new friends was spiralling out of control?

'It didn't take long before I was funding all of our habits.' Jenny continued. *'Their demands grew daily straining my monthly allowance. I continued attending my weekly sessions because if I hadn't, it would raise concerns and my Father would cease the drip feed allowance.'*

Before she even said it, I knew what she was about to say. In her delusional mind, she knew there was only one thing she could do and that was to sell her home and purchase another, a smaller one. The property sold quickly due to a reduced price.

I could feel the difficulty she had in revealing the fact to me that she knew she was being taken advantage of. They abused her good and generous nature. At last, the penny had dropped. Her new-found friends had deserted her, and very rapidly once they knew the wishing well had run dry. A new property was never purchased. She was broke, homeless and an alcoholic with a drug addiction. At her lowest ebb, she hated the fact she had to admit defeat to her family as she had nowhere else to go. A few months had passed. Jenny was back home and attending further counselling groups for addiction. Her mind was still playing tricks.

I felt we were still short of where we needed to be. We had only scratched a bit of the detail that I was looking for. I asked, *'So, your back home with your family and doing counselling for your addictions. What happened next?'*
Jenny responded, *'That's right. This is when the "really weird stuff" started to happen. Looking at it now, this is about the time when my eating habits started changing and they changed dramatically. I suddenly began to crave the desire to eat meat. This is strange as I'd been a vegetarian for most of my life. I became more lethargic and couldn't be bothered by my appearance. It was far too time-consuming in doing so. Being back with the family was making me feel claustrophobic and oppressed. It was everything Id fought to get away from and I was back. I realised and could see for myself, I was in a desperate way, mentally and emotionally.'*
This was better. We were finally getting to a point of clear transition.

Jenny then said, *'I became cunning and realised the best way to release my boredom in my weekly sessions was to act out a role. I gave an academy award performance and pretend the counselling was having an impact on me.'* I realised this was the first time Jenny had spoken with a tone, not as the voice of a victim, but rather the perpetrator. This was a new slant on things. She got my attention.

As if to start slowly prodding her, I asked *'So, you deluded the therapist into believing the sessions were working.'*

'Yes, I now relished in my weekly meetings acting out what was expected.' She replied as if smug about her accomplishment. *'It was deceitful, but it gave me control and some joy. I was bored. No one was listening or taking me seriously.'*

I could physically see a change in character. She had a pride about her deception. In her cockiness, Jenny was revealing probably more than she realised. She was trying to treat me in the same manner. She said, *'The voice I hear in my head would mock the councillor, repeating word for word what she had said. It was becoming increasingly difficult not to laugh out loud as I thought it amusing. As a result of my brilliant acting skills, my medication was reduced.'*

My patience was starting to pay off as she continued, *'My family were relieved and seemed pleased with the councillor's progress, I just kept quiet. As time went on, I began to experience what is best described as blackouts, but without losing consciousness. This started to happen to me with regular frequency and it was during these memory lapses that others had commented that I would demonstrate great bouts of anger and physical abuse. I couldn't remember anything and held no responsibility for my actions. My mother felt she could no longer accompany me whilst out shopping or during some other menial task'*

I asked, *'So you experienced an aggressive manner only during these blackouts?' 'Yes.'* She replied. *'In one incident, I was just coming around from such a blackout to realise I had pinned my Mother up against the wall in a shopping centre. I'd assaulted her and was shocked to see her face bruised with her bottom lip bleeding. What was happening to me? Was I going mad?'*

In my mind, I was trying the find the border between, Schizophrenia or paranormal, where did one end and the other begin. Did one exist or both? A pattern was forming, and one that I was very familiar with.

Jenny stated *'The voices in my head were telling me to do things; harmful things. I'd convinced everyone that I was on the mend and that I'd continue attending my weekly sessions. I gained the trust of my Mother and went by myself, unchaperoned. Over time I'd begun to bunk off these sessions as they were now becoming boring and repetitive. I felt there was something inside me that wanted more.'* Even Jenny's demeanour was showing one of boredom. *'As time went on it became apparent to my parents that I had not been going to my classes as the councillor had informed them of my lack of attendance.'*

I could physically see her desire when she stated that she had a longing that was so strong and deep within her to see and meet up with the vagrant's group. What was driving this desire when they clearly weren't her friends.

One evening, she had found herself standing outside her former home. One member, of the vagrant group, recognised her and approached her. Tom was the youngest and the most intelligent of them. She never did find out why he had ended up on the streets. He wanted to apologise to her for their behaviour as he knew they hadn't treated her well and they had taken advantage of her. During their conversation, Tom brought up that their vagrant group was no longer together. An incident had occurred a few months back that lead to them moving off their patch. When Jenny asked what had happened, Tom said, *'A scuffle with a rival gang had turned nasty. Michael was stabbed. A local resident had called the police, but it was too late for Michael. He had died on the spot where he fell.'* Jenny was absolutely devastated, *'Looking back now, I can see this was the time when I'd lost control. I was spiralling down into a deep dark pit with an unknown destination.'*

Jenny was trying to put the pieces together in her mind. *'Just recently I've begun experiencing consecutive dreams, they're really vivid, but it feels like I'm not fully asleep. The face of a man comes into view, but it's like seeing him in a dense fog. His face looks distorted. I feel as if he is arguing with me and seems very agitated. I get confused and can't make out what his says. I can feel his displeasure with me, but I don't know why?'*

I felt these were not dreams; she was experiencing astral visits. She had both feet in my world and it was time to shake the tree a bit more and see what falls out. I had to be mindful of the fact she had been through this entire ordeal and was still coming off the influence of substances. There was also the possibility she could still be unpredictable with her Schizophrenia. I asked, *'Try and remember a little more detail, as best as you can.'*

She replied, *'He's a young man in his mid-thirties with dark piercing eyes. I feel there's something very familiar about him.'*

We had arrived at the reveal. I felt very strongly there was just the one entity at play here. It was a male. He was matching the description I had jotted down prior to her arrival. I'd sensed he had a motive. It was a sinister plan that required her energies to manipulate and claim them as his own. A real sense of foreboding came over me as I realised he required her to carry out an act on his behalf.

Jenny had been a perfect host who offered very little if any resistance. I asked her, *'These voices you hear in your head, can you tell me if there are many different voices or just the one?'*

She said, *'No. Only one. It's a man's voice. It's always the same. Do you know what's strange? Somehow, it sounds somewhat familiar.'*

I knew she was trying to perform her actress of the year performance on me. However, I could see right through to the understudy that was pulling the strings. My eyes were now fixed upon Jenny; waiting and watching for the right time to play my hand. I said in a voice of which to call her bluff, *'Oh come on Michael…'*

Out of my peripheral vision, I could see Shaun shoot me a look. He then looked to Jenny, and then back at me. With a look of concern on his face, he was trying to figure out what he missed. Jenny took up a cocky body position in the chair as if to suggest she was still in control. Her whole demeanour had changed. I felt the entities energy was here. He was in my home and sitting right opposite me. My thoughts became more alert to my own surroundings. I could sense my guides protection around me.

She glanced up at me, giving me a strained smile. However, superseded by her own facial features was a momentary glimpse of what I believed to be the entities glare. I asked myself, *'Did she just have a glitch?'* I looked at her boyfriend for any sign of validation of what I had witnessed. There was no reaction. I knew then that Michael had revealed himself to me.

During our conversation, I'd noticed Jenny's posture had begun to change. She suddenly took up a bolt upright position in her chair. She was moving her body closer to the edge of her seat. Michael was assuming a challenging stance to Jenny's posture. She had an icy glare about her that was directed towards me. I believe it was in the hope of trying to intimidate me. I remained calm and held my contact with her. Partly camouflaged within Jenny's aura, I could see the dark shadow of the entity. I could feel his intense anger towards me.

She moved with a twitching action and then had remained still, like a statue. My full focus and concentration were on her. I hadn't ever witnessed this before. At first, I thought it a case of Tourette's. However, the energy Id felt, assured me, it was far more. Throughout the latter part of the conversation, Michael would periodically override her features. His vibration was a dark force. These beings are generally more negative and destructive than the other spirits mentioned. They cause deeper and more serious issues in the people they possess They generally go to great lengths to obtain what they seek.

Over a period of time, Michael would have slowly manipulated her energy until she became so weak and vulnerable that she would be open to the possession. She will experience mental and emotional memories encountered by the etheric blueprint, totally changing the personality of the new host's body. Eventually, it would affect Jenny on a physical level. His aim was ultimately to orchestrate her actions as his own.

Jenny's agitation grew, her body language and facial features conveyed stress.

What's happening, Jenny? What's' going on?' I asked as she became very angry and disorientated. She stood up, scraping her chair back away from the table. I looked at her with authority and complete control, asking, *'Are you going somewhere?'* Shaun stood up, but it was more out of confusion. He looked at me for direction as to what to do next. I waved my hand at him to sit back down. She followed Shaun's example and sat back down. It looked very much like an internal battle was taking place Jenny versus Michael.

Still calm and letting things reveal themselves, I gave Jenny more to think about, *'What happened just then, Jenny? What did you feel?'*

'Revenge. An eye for an eye, for the scum who took me down.' Although spoken in Jenny's own voice, the words were Michael's. I believed this was the moment in time when Michael had taken full control over Jenny. He was manipulating her thoughts, desires and actions.

It was at this stage that I showed Jenny the sketch I had drawn prior to their arrival. She flinched as soon as she saw the dagger with the serpent twisting around its blade. She shot me a cold look. I raised my voice very slightly

97

talking directly through to Michael with an expectation he would fully reveal himself. *'Michael was your life taken by another's hand and is it revenge you seek? Do you require Jenny to finish off your business? Is this what this is all about?* Jenny looked at me frowning, her expression was one of shock. I continued explaining, 'Michael's life had been taken by the thrusting of a knife deep into his stomach, *isn't that so Michael?'*

I'd addressed Jenny, *'I feel Michael lost his life as a result of a brawl over drugs. Jenny, he wants you to take this man's life in revenge. He knows his murderer continues to walk the streets. The dagger tattoo is imprinted upon the hand of his killer and this was the last image Michael had seen. It connects to the man he now hunts.'*

I paused for a moment for her to digest what I had told her and take in what I was about to tell her. *'Michael has been manipulating your mind into thinking a certain way. This has been done over time. This was done so you would carry out his dirty deed for him. He knows who he is searching for. With the right conditions, he will use your physical hand and manipulate your actions. The strong emotions of unfinished business are so great within Michael that he feels he cannot cross over. He wants Justice.'*

You could see Jenny was struggling to take it on in when she responded, *'You mean I have Michael, my Michael affecting me, working through me as such? He wants me to find his killer and take his life. This is just so bizarre, even for my ears.'* She began to laugh out loud. She stood up as if dismissing the idea of such a fantasy. However, Shaun refrained her from doing so. You could tell from his expression he was piecing these fragments of information together.

Shaun spoke, *'I can take what you're saying on board, but Jenny was experiencing strange things prior to Michaels death. It doesn't add up.'*

'Let me try and explain.' I said in a voice that was calm and of experience. *'Jenny is a natural clairsentient. She has and will always be ultra -sensitive to spirit. In her previous family home, the new- build, although other members of the family witnessed "strange stuff" as Jenny would call it, she seemed to be the only one who was affected by it.'*

Being a sensitive, Jenny saw and experienced more than others. Jenny has in no way had a spirit attachment or a haunting. She just had a very active environment. Being depressed, regardless of the cause, is the start of having a low energy vibration. Being unhappy and living in a household whose religious beliefs she felt, was fanatical caused a great oppression in her.'

This was proving difficult for Shaun to digest as he said, *'I don't get it; how can this Michael get inside Jenny?'*

I responded, *'When we deplete our energies on all aspects as Jenny had on a mental, emotional and physical element and together with being highly sensitive, is a cocktail looking for its extra fizz. She was not trained or versed in the ways of protection. She had never been exposed to anything of this nature before. The energy field, or aura as its most commonly known, thins and depletes offering easy access for passing negative energies.'*

Jenny pipped up, *'So, the dream state I experienced, was that Michael?'*

'Yes.' I replied. *'I believe he showed himself to you in your mind as a way of scaring you off and trying to prevent you from attending this meeting. By you coming here, he would fear his existence on the earth plain could be in jeopardy.'*

Jenny commented, ok so *'I'm keeping him alive to an extent then? He's utilising my physical energy, like a vampire? That would explain why I'm becoming so weak?'*

'That correct.' I said. *'This also explains your out of character antics. Schizophrenia was the perfect diagnosis to camouflage what*

was happening. It does make me wonder if many other people are being utilised as hosts and labelled with a medical condition. You very often hear the words from a serial killer saying, the voices in my head tell me to kill!'

You could see from Jenny's expression she was starting to understand how it all fits together and stated, *'It's starting to make sense now. Iv been a vegetarian for many years not eating meat and yet I craved for it. This is a lot for me to get my head around.*

I broke the news that we still had one more step to complete, *'It's time to separate energies. Michael needs to move on with his spiritual journey.'* I saw the real Jenny reflected within her downcast eyes. She looked up and nodded her agreement to whatever she had to do.

I stated firmly, *'I'm going to perform the cleanse. Please try and remain seated.'* I was already tuned into my guides and they were fully aware of the procedure. I am but a tiny cog in a big mechanism that deals with such matters.

Jenny asked, *'Will the cleans hurt him?'* The concern in Jenny's voice was alarming.

I couldn't believe what I was hearing and said, *'He stole your life for his own. He didn't think twice about his actions which were for himself only. He had wanted you to murder for him, so he could claim justice. He used you then as he is doing so now and yet you worry how it may affect him!'*

Shaun shot her a contemptuous look but said nothing. She got the message it was sent with.

I explained to them both of the protective circle of light that I would surround them in whilst carrying out the cleanse, as per my normal procedure. I had received permission from Jenny to go ahead. After some instruction, Jenny was to visualize a technique I had given her in order to focus her mind.

Whilst connecting with my guides, I had asked they bring forth the spirit rescue team who are highly evolved spirits. They work on lost soul retrieval. They escort the souls to where they will receive a form of counselling.

During this process, with my eyes closed, I had felt a grabbing to my arm. Jenny had seized me in a strong-arm lock, her face was tinged with fear and yet held an undercurrent of defiance. I knew Michael was reluctant to go and Jenny was having a hard time in releasing him.

With authority, I said, *Let him go, Jenny. He will receive the help and assistance he requires.'*
Just at that precise moment, there was an almighty flash of light, engulfing the whole room. It was breath-taking. There are no words that come to mind in even hoping to explain the feeling we felt. Jenny began to sob uncontrollably.

Michael was met and had been received into the light. He would be assisted to continue his spiritual journey.

Summary:
Jenny had sent me word that she was feeling much healthier and was in control of her life and was feeling more like her own self once more. She was continuing to re-build her connection with her family. She told me she had felt at peace.

Chapter 6

The Pitted Mirror

Several years ago, a foreign woman, of Hungarian descent living in England, was having an argument over the phone with her alcoholic father, who resided in Hungary. Relations between them had always been one of struggle. With his destructive addiction, he continually leant on his family for financial support. This phone conversation started no different from any of the rest. As the exchange grew more heated, out of frustration, she told her father, "You're just a waste of space and a burden on the family. Why don't you do everyone a favour; just go and end it all." Her father went missing shortly thereafter. It was found she was the last one to have spoken with him.

Three months later, high up in isolated hills, hikers had found her father's body in a cave. Obviously, at a low point and heavily under the influence, he must have felt he had no other way out of his torment. He had taken his own life and no longer wanted to be that burden. Not only was the suicide devastating to her, but her family had learnt from the last conversation he had, had. They blamed and ostracized her for his actions.

With her family living in Hungary and feeling like her husband didn't fully comprehend or understand her pain, she had no one to talk too. Her loneliness grew as did her despair. The seed of guilt firmly set, she was desperate to get some form of contact and forgiveness from her father. She turned to several mediums for a spiritual connection in the hope that he would come through; he never did. With each reading, her desperation became greater.

Some time had passed, her obsession was growing and getting out of control. She was determined to have contact with her father. She obtained a Ouija board and would sit alone in her bedroom practising daily and yet, he still didn't come through. Desperately she took a step further and purchased a spell book learning how to recite rituals and working with the occult with no concern or understanding as to what else was going on around her...

Mark lived in his home with his second wife who was heavily pregnant, along with their 15-month old boy.

They were often awoken in the early hours of the morning by their toddler's screams and had heard strange noises coming from their son's intercom speakers placed in his bedroom. They could hear the voice of an angry male. The voice so clear they thought there must be an intruder.

Both running into his room, they witnessed seeing his toys had had a life of their own. The boy's favourite toy, a wind-up Donald Duck, was waddling and quacking from one end of the room to the other. His police car, with blue flashing lights, was moving around and around in circles while the musical mobile, above his cot, of which had also been activated, constantly repeated the phrase "the cow jumped over the moon."

Grabbing their son from his cot, they had great difficulty in consoling him. Naturally being so young and not yet able to voice his plight, he simply pointed and stared at a corner of his room with a fearful expression upon his face, looking anxiously at his mother and father in the hope of being understood. The room had felt cold cool breezes would just appear no matter how high the heating.

Mark was also experiencing strange phenomena on a regular basis. Work tools, saws, hammers, and the like, would simply disappear from the place he had last left them only to then be found somewhere else, days later, in the strangest of places. The fridge, oven and toy box seemed to be the most favoured. On some occasions, tools would just disappear within minutes of using them and of which were placed right beside him at the time.

The list of phenomenal happenings is vast, but they include ornaments on the shelves that would fly across the room at some speed. Books have been witnessed by friends and neighbours to fall off the bookcase one by one in a row as if an invisible hand was running along the shelf. On one occasion, a friend of Mark's who was visiting at the time had witnessed a pen materialise in mid-air and thrown forcefully at Mark from the other side of the room. The odour of strong tobacco smoke is often smelt and many times, a tall shadowy figure has been seen going up the stairs, across the landing and entering the child's room.

His wife too experienced strange things. She often felt the strong presence of someone standing close beside her especially whilst she lay in bed. She would shake Mark to awaken him because she was so frightened. On several occasions, they could both clearly see a depression forming beside her as if someone had sat down. Strange scratching sounds, like that of clawing fingernails, as described by Mark, are distinctly heard coming from inside the wardrobe. As though someone or something was trying to find release. The taps and bangs were so forceful at times, they believed the wardrobe would topple over on top of them.

The pattern of events became more intense and with it more startling. His wife would be awoken by the sudden vibration and movement of the bed. She awoke abruptly with disbelief as she witnessed seeing Mark's head being pulled backwards and forwards bashing his head repeatedly against the wooden bed rail. He seemed powerless to stop it or defend himself. He would wince out in pain as long red scratches appeared on his neck and chest.

Mark had no understanding or previous experience of this phenomena, He wanted it to stop so his life could resume back to some form of normality. He was advised by friends to contact a church for help. He obtained my telephone number from his local Spiritualist Church where my name is listed as a contact in cases of paranormal activity. It was whilst speaking with him on the phone, discussing my request that his pregnant wife and young toddler weren't to be at the location during my visit as a prerequisite to make sure, should anything happen, they weren't in any danger. In mid-sentence, I suddenly heard a crashing sound with Mark giving a surprised scream of concern...

Gail – *"What's happening, Mark?"*
Mark – With panic in his voice. *"The carousel spice rack is turning around by itself and the jars are flying out towards me!"*
Gail – *"Are you okay?*
Mark – *"It's on the opposite side of the kitchen to where I'm standing and it's throwing jars at me..."*
Gail – *"Get out of there?"*
Mark – *"I can't. The phone is attached to the wall."*
Gail – *"Okay, hang up and I'll see you Thursday.*

As Mark didn't have any other form of communication at that time other than his wall phone I didn't want to put him at risk trying to contact him again. We didn't speak again until the day of our appointment.

From my works as a Physical Medium, I had gained interest from a small film company. They knew I had taken this case and had wanted to accompany me.

The film crew had already arrived at the location and were there to greet me. They hadn't entered the house so that we could all go in together. Walking through the threshold of the front door, my guides had instructed me that I needed to investigate the child's room first and foremost.

After a very brief greeting with Mark, the crew of 4 went into the lounge to set up their electrical equipment. I went in the opposite direction, proceeding up the narrow staircase I knew exactly where I was to go as my guides were directing me towards the toddler's bedroom.

Upon entering, I could feel the icy coldness of the room together with a familiar earthy smell, confirming the remnant of ectoplasm. Something had been here very recently leaving behind this residue of energy. My focus and concentration were upon the cot. I could feel myself being pulled, towards the little bed. The vibrational pull was so great, I experienced the sensation like that of being on a boat when it rocked from side to side, causing a little disorientation and light headiness.

I knew this feeling well, it was an indication to me of a portal opening, often described as an invisible gateway to other realms. A place where dark forces can easily come and go at will and slip through, as uninvited guests.

It was whilst in the toddler's room, that the camera crew along with Mark had joined me. During my time alone, I had formed a spiritual communication with a gentleman using telepathic thought to communicate. I was informed he was Mark's paternal grandfather and that the two had been very close during his life.

It was quite unusual to strike up a connection with a loved one's family member during the process of a cleanse. He gave his name to me when asked. Spirit validation is a vital part of my work. I simply relay to the client what I am hearing in my mind repeating exactly as I receive it, without my own interpretation or elaboration. I'm mindful of not altering the original intended message. He spoke of dates of the importance of which Mark validated. Also of shared memories, some of which had been forgotten about until mentioned. Other family member's names, both here, still on the earth plane and those that have crossed over, were given as further validation. Mark had felt less frightened, in the knowledge his beloved grandfather was assisting him and doing all that was possible to help him from his realm.

His grandfather was acting as a spectator, communicating with me throughout the whole process. He was teaching me that loving spirits do not enter the same space or dimension as that of the "lower" entities because they reside in a different vibrational space. However, they are very aware of each other's presence. It is always advisable that a physical medium who specialises in this form of energy is to be present with their spirit guides, who work together for such a clearing to take place.

Acting under Grandfather's guidance I was further instructed to go to the bathroom. Through our mental communication, I'd heard the words *"the pitted mirror."* Being unsure of what I had heard, I'd asked him can *you please repeat what you have just said.* I was speaking out loud so that Mark and the crew would be able to at least follow half the conversation giving them an idea as to where we were headed.

The spirit of the grandfather would not enter the bathroom, saying he could not share the same space as the lower entity. The bathroom was a small room and only had adequate space for Mark and myself. The crew had to remain just outside the door.

Upon the bathroom wall hung a large mirror of which had shown many pitted marks due to its age. This must have been to what the grandfather had referred to.

I could sense we were not alone and knew we were being watched.

Mark was feeling apprehensive but had followed me into the bathroom. The crews sound boom, resembling an oversized feather duster, was held out of view, so as not to capture its reflection.

I stood for a while facing the mirror not knowing what to expect. I could see Marks reflection standing directly behind me. Something caught my attention, another figure had come into view. I'd seen a tall dark swarthy-skinned man with a heavy brow. This must be the entity, revealing himself, however, I am not sure this was intentional. Just as I was about to reveal what I was seeing, Mark suddenly fell backwards, his hair had been vigorously pulled, knocking him off balance.

The crew all quickly dispersed in response as they witnessed seeing Mark fall backwards with force.

Bringing my eyes and attention back to the mirror, I saw deeply reflected in its image, the bottom of a large bed, with a purple cover draped upon it. I was transfixed and commentated out aloud for all to hear. As the scene became more intensified I could clearly see the pattern on the carpet and walls. I'd noticed a large book placed at the end of the bed and a Ouija board was sat on a small table that stood beside it.

Mark confirmed the decoration of the room as I'd described. He remarked it was his previous matrimonial bedroom, and of what is now being currently used by his son. The images revealed within the mirror were of a distant past when he was married to his Hungarian wife and of the space where she conducted her daily ritual. He also remarked this mirror was, in fact, the only remaining piece of property belonging to her, that had remained in the home.

Communication from his grandfather interjected with me again and suggested I enter the master bedroom. He informed me the entity was present within. I knew he was correct the moment we entered the room. The negative energy once inside was so prevalent. The oppression I'd felt was very heavy, the crew remarked they too could feel it. Mark once again was the entities focus. He became very disorientated and reached out his arms to steady himself. He sat down on the edge of the bed for support, his breathing laboured. He seemed to be struggling for breath and with a panicked look on his face, began to scratch wildly at his neck as if to loosen his collar. I had asked Mark to concentrate on his breathing. Relaxing his intake and exhale of breath.

The film crew had followed us from room to room, taking pictures. They were in the process of setting up a camera on a tripod at the bottom of the bed and were just adjusting its height when the bed began to vibrate so much so, the legs banged violently upon the floor. At times, the bed had risen completely. Poor Mark, shot me a look with total fear held within his eyes.

The crew were shocked to be witnessing this and were experiencing unusual power failure to their equipment. Their backup battery pack had also failed. One by one the crew had started to feel sick and had to leave the room abruptly.

I was unsure of what might have been the next attack and wanted to diffuse its anger. I'd called out to him in a calm voice. I wanted to strike up a form of communication with him. There was no response.

Mark and I remained sitting on the bed, neither of us spoke. I could see he was very physically shaken and his pallor very pale, he was on the point of collapse. I'd mentally called out to my spirit team to come in to assist as I didn't feel he could take much more. Very shortly thereafter the rocking and vibrating of the bed had begun to calm. I knew my spirit rescue team were doing what they do best. By the atmosphere change, I knew the situation was under control.

Mark eventually spoke in a cracked voice saying '" *Has all this happened because of my ex-wife's using that Ouija board and bloody spell book"*? Yes, I had remarked explaining that without the proper protection and knowledge of what she was practising she had unknowingly opened a portal between two worlds.

I explained Ouija boards are used as a communication device to connect to another dimension. In the right hands and correct environment, they can be used safely to contact spirits that reside in the higher realms. In the wrong hands, a high-risk situation can occur with the potential of attracting troubled entities.

This is exactly what had happened. In the same way a moth is attracted to a light. I explained my role in the cleanse in that I am used as a 'source of power'. A physical medium is necessary to be present to allow this in order for the cleanse to take place. I am just a very small cog in the wheel for the spirit rescue team to do their work.

I have come to find that holy water and smudging is not always an effective method of clearances.

My thoughts went to the crew and had hoped they were all ok.

Summary:
A few weeks after the cleanse, Mark called to give me an update. They were celebrating the birth of their second son.

The house is quiet and peaceful with no further incidents.

Chapter 7

The Anniversary Ghost

It was cold, afternoon in October. My daughter, Kelly, had asked for me to pick her up from her place of work at a country golf hotel in Hertfordshire. She had finished her shift, working on reception, and her car had refused to start.

Coming off the A1 and onto a roundabout, I took the first exit onto a small b road that runs through a small village. The golf club is located a few miles further up the road. For the most point, the journey had been pretty uneventful and there wasn't much traffic about.

I had driven this route several times, the road was very familiar to me. Following a very slight bend in the road, I began to feel a slowly growing vibration run through my body that felt like I was being warned. As the vibration increased, it felt the same as when my spiritual senses alert me to a spirit entity's presence. I turned off the radio and came off the accelerator, as I wanted to be vigilant, concentrating on my internal feelings placing me on full alert.

I'd started looking at the dashboard of my car to see if it was highlighting a warning sign. I glanced over my shoulder and in the rear-view mirror could see there was no one in the back or passenger seat. Fields lay to my left and to my right was an empty pedestrian path that led down towards the village pub. My side mirrors were also clear. The place was desolate with no one else in sight. I was the only car on the road. The vibration I was feeling was becoming stronger. I checked my speed dial and noted I was doing around 20mph at this time.

For a second, I'd thought to myself "They (my guides) must be making a mistake." My logical mind was trying to make sense of the situation of why I was feeling these impressions. Arguing with myself, I knew to trust my spiritual senses. Something was about to happen but I had no idea what!

Before finishing my last thought, something appeared in my peripheral view catching my attention. Glancing to my right to see what it was, an image of a man's face was looking through my window straight at me. His face was almost pressed against the glass. It startled me for a brief second as I had already looked there, but I didn't swerve and just continued at my set speed.

I'd looked again and could see he was actually running beside the car. His expression looked as though he was taunting me. He had a menacing grin. He was so close I could make out his features in detail. He had damp reddish blonde hair and the palest of blue eyes. His skin was slightly freckled. He was dressed in jogging attire, wearing a white vest top with red piping and red shorts. His face was red which I could only put down to exertion.

Many distorted thoughts flooded through my mind while I tried to make sense and comprehend what was happening while keeping my eyes on the road. Then, coming from just in my peripheral, with a sudden burst of speed, he shot forward and ran straight in front of my car.

In a split second, the most horrific feeling came over me as I immediately slammed on my brakes, but wasn't quick enough. The car jolted to the thud on impact. I had hit him. I struggle to explain the feeling and emotion that is experienced when you think you have hit someone. The closest I can say is that I felt physically sick, drained of energy and afraid. All of this happened as if time had suddenly stood still creating a real surreal moment and one I'd never experienced before.

With my car stopped and emergency brake on, I sat motionless with my body physically shaking and my mind frantic with thought. My hands were gripped tightly on the steering wheel, so much so I could see the whiteness of my knuckles. I knew I was in shock. I was trying to convince myself to let go of the steering wheel. Nausea had started to set in with disbelief of what had just happened, I couldn't move. I was scared to get out and look under my car.

Sitting for what felt like an eternity, I took a deep breath and slowly got out of the car. I was still very much alone on the road. Images wouldn't stop flooding my mind with the horrible possibilities of what I might find. Preparing myself, with a pounding heart, I took a few steps forward ...

It was that moment when you had to look but you don't want to see. Telling myself to be brave, I looked at the front end of the driver's side of the car ... I couldn't see anything. I took another step forward, seeing a lot more of the front bumper and noticing there was no damage. Now in front of the car, still nothing. I gingerly bent down to take a look underneath. Nothing! No body, no blood, no dents.

Still shaking, I examined the car for any possible signs of impact. There were none. Trying to make sense of what had occurred, I stood up onto the inset of my door to gain extra height so I could have a good view across the fields just in case there was any possibility he may have crawled out from underneath the car or been thrown, but nothing.

After not being able to find anything and feeling drained, I sat down in the car. I'd needed to take a few minutes to compose myself before continuing to drive. I was so relieved but had a feeling of being battered. For the rest of the journey, I couldn't stop talking out-loud to myself.

Reaching the golf club, I had to walk inside to let my daughter know that I'd arrived. When she saw me, she asked if I was ok

Kelly: "You're as white as ash mum. You okay?"

Gail: "No not really, not at all."
Kelly: What's the matter? What's happened?"
Gail: "I think I've just killed someone..."
Kelly: "What do you mean mum?" Looking worried.
Gail: "I've just run someone over."

Kelly asked for a member of staff, Ingrid, to get me a cup of coffee.

Coming back with the coffee, Ingrid heard me telling Kelly about the accident. Ingrid had been an employee at the hotel for almost 18 years. She told us in her German accent,

"You know, several guests on their drive up to this hotel have also experienced the same phenomena. Same location too. What month is this?" she asked herself. "October, that's right, always in October. I have heard this same story on at least 6 other occasions."

Ingrid also confirmed the description of the jogger, together with the details of the incident, were the same as mine.

Summary:

To my relief, I knew what had happened. I explained this phenomenon was known as an anniversary haunting. These types of residual hauntings are where ghosts are seen on the anniversary of their death, basically a recorded image or a replay of certain events. These recordings are thought to be imprints left over from strong emotions and generally referred to as 'Anniversary Ghosts'. The spirit of a person returns to appear on the same day, at the same time, in the same place, year after year.

I'd tried researching old archives and the internet of any reported accidents on that stretch of road that had matched my experience but unfortunately, I couldn't find any mention about it. With so little to go on and his style of clothing giving no timings, it was very difficult to put it in a specific time frame of when it had actually occurred.

Although this incident had lasted for minutes only, it has left a lingering impression upon me and not one that I can easily forget.

Chapter 8
The Other Side

The depth of the love from a parent for their children cannot be measured. It is like no other relationship. It is said to be one of the most special bonds a human can possess. Sadly, I am not alone to have experienced your child to predecease you. I have read for many women who have also lost a child and of whom I have been instrumental in clarifying, their transition into the spirit realm, as I understand it.

These children are well-developed souls and may require only a short contact with the earth in order for them to spiritually progress. We as their parents have been chosen specifically for this transaction to take place. They come to us for a short while in order to experience the love we can give them, before returning once again to a better place.

I have an understanding that babies who have terminated their contract during pregnancy and have passed as a result of miscarriage when on the other side will be looked after and brought up my relatives of that child, together with specifically trained spirit nurses and nannies. Their environment will be childlike with beautiful surroundings. The child will be told about their parents and will continue to grow and develop as they would have done here. I truly believe we will be reunited in heaven.

What follows is my own experience when my daughter returned home.

It was whilst visiting my mother one Saturday afternoon with my then husband and two daughters, that my life had changed forever.

My youngest daughter Claire had been happily playing with her sister on the other side of the room when she suddenly jumped up and turned around and stared at me with a look of shock on her tiny face. She began to walk towards me, calling out mummy. She fell into my arms and became very limp and unresponsive.

Something was seriously wrong; my heart had sunk as I watched her life force begin to drain from her. Her eyes dulled and began to close, very slowly. This was the last time I would see her almost black eyes, staring back at mine.

My mind could not, would not, accept the reality. Claire had died peacefully in my arms. I began to give resuscitation but knew it was fruitless as she had already gone.

My husband had made the inevitable call to the emergency services. An ambulance had arrived some minutes later. They checked eye and pulse reactions and said nothing, they didn't need to.

There had to be a police report as she had been a home death and an autopsy was carried out especially as she was or had seemed to be, healthy and presenting no medical conditions. It was discovered she had a congenital heart condition known as cardiomyopathy. I did not know she had been born with this condition. The muscles in her heart were too weak and it became apparent that once she got older and had become more physically active, it had proven too much of a strain on her heart.

My world as I had known it was over. Things were never going to be the same again. Inside my mind, I was screaming No. It's just a dream and I will wake up and find it had never happened. The physical pain I experienced had ripped through my heart piercing it to its core.

I was angry at God for taking her. I didn't want anything to do with my guides who had drawn close to me to console me, I could feel their presence. I closed down physically and mentally to them and told them to bugger off and leave me alone. I no longer wanted to be an evolved soul or to experience all things in order to understand and reach out to others along my path. I wanted to be normal and live a normal life.

Over the coming months, I had retreated into myself and became a recluse, stuck in my own grief.

My health had been deteriorating to such a degree that my mother had stayed at my home, helping my husband with our eldest daughter. He had reluctantly returned to work and was trying to get back to some sort of normality.

It was whilst I was resting on the sofa, that an extraordinary thing happened. I began to feel extremely heavy and lethargic and just had to close my eyes. I felt as if I was drifting deeper and deeper, feeling myself becoming heavier and heavier, an extreme calmness had washed over me. I became aware of my body vibrating the slightest of moves with a sensation of sliding forward as if I was on a slow-moving conveyor belt. I was leaving my body, feet first. I did not struggle but just surrendered to it.

There was a very brief moment of darkness before the grey eyes of a gentleman with silvery hair came into view. He was sat beside me. I did not recognise him but somehow, I'd felt I knew him. Claire was lying on a stretcher and wrapped in a red blanket. Looking around me, I knew we were sitting in an ambulance as I could clearly see all things familiar.

She was not receiving medical assistance. I'd turned to look at the man beside me and asked who he was and what was happening? He told me his name was Richard and that he was a Doctor. He said he had come to help me. Our communication was entirely by telepathy.

We came to a stop and upon getting out; I followed the stretcher into the hospital. Richard and I walked side by side down a long stretch of the corridor until we came to a swing door with two Perspex windowpanes.

Claire went ahead and was wheeled through these doors but I was stopped by Richard. He raised his hands barring my exit through the doorway. He spoke to me saying I was not to enter but just to observe.

He told me I had gone as far as permitted. You are just to observe he repeated. I didn't understand what was happening and wanted to know where they had taken Claire. I looked through the viewing pane and into the room. I could see many people. They were all wearing white medical gowns and had their heads bent down and were gathered around her stretcher.

The crowd began to disperse and took a step back. I could see they had turned around to look in my direction. Richard told me to look closely. The red blanket had been removed, I could see that placed on the side, next to the trolley. A young woman with dark hair was sitting upright. Her eyes looked straight into mine. We were able to connect mentally. Telepathically I could hear her voice in my mind. I knew this was Claire. She was projecting herself to me in an adult form.

I was confused but then gained comfort as she went on to tell me that I had been chosen by her, to be her mother. She had wanted us to share this experience together. She explained our path had been written and there was nothing that could have prevented this chapter in our lives.

She informed me she had not suffered any pain and that she was an old soul and that she will join me when it is my time, to make the transition. She smiled at me and looked so at peace which had eased some of the pain within my broken heart.

I am not sure I fully understood all she had said, or why she had presented her image to me as a grown woman but I knew and felt it was her. I turned to Richard beside me, looking for answers. I had wanted him to do all that was within his power to change things. I told him I wanted Claire back and that I no longer wanted to walk this path I had chosen. I wanted out.

I pushed hard on the door to which Richard interjected saying this isn't permitted.

He began to tell me that I would bare a son in the future and not to be afraid. He would be strong, a survivor. What do you mean by that, my mind had screeched out at him? I did not want to hear about any other future children I just wanted this nightmare to end.

I was prepared to suffer the consequences of my actions so pushed harder at it; I felt the release of the door and also a pain to my face. My focus seemed intent on the pain I was experiencing and had removed my hands from the door to cup my head.

I opened my eyes to my mother smacking me hard around my face and shaking me vigorously to awaken me. I could hear her frantic voice yelling at me "come back, you must not leave, you're needed here". I was being reprimanded. I remember feeling a bump as if I had knocked into something with the sensation of my body becoming heavy once more. I realised Richard was no longer beside me and all I'd wanted to do was to return to the warm darkness where I had felt safe.

I explained to my mother all that I had seen and of the meeting with Richard. She was shocked at the mention of his name. Describe how he looked, she had asked. I gave her his in-depth description. She gasped an intake of breath and smiled. *"Do you know who he was*, I'd asked? *Is he my new guide"?* She replied no his mine.

Summary:
My mother and I had parted ways when I was a young girl and for many years I did not know of her whereabouts, we had no connection. When I became a teenage wife and mother myself, I reunited with her. I'd found out she had resided in St Hellier Jersey. She had informed me Richard had wanted to be the one who took me to the other side, to meet with Claire. I was confused and had so many questions to ask I didn't know how to feel or where to begin. Being a natural Medium herself, she was able to inform me on many spiritual matters concerning the conditioning for children in the spirit realm.

Richard's name was mentioned only once after this incidence, a couple of years later, whilst my mother was on her deathbed. She was dying of lung cancer. I had nursed her until the end and would spend many an evening talking through the night.

Richard had come for her. I knew her belief had helped her to cope and surrender herself to the light.

This experience did help with my recovery. I also remembered Richards words to me that I would go on and bare a son. I now also understood the comment he had made with regards to him being strong.

During my scans throughout my pregnancy, it was shown that Steven had a hole in his heart. Thankfully it was in the soft muscle and the prognosis was good. He was not to partake in any contact sport and was to be extremely careful whilst in his youth. In time, the hole began to close and heal. He is now a strapping healthy young man.

His elder sister Kelly had also been checked over and was given the all-clear. I was sterilised by the age of 24 but was thankful for having my two children.

Chapter 9
The Souls Journey

Many people have asked me about their purpose in life, as in "why was I born"? There is a mass awareness that is occurring that wasn't available to us 20 years ago. Times have changed to where we can challenge those institutions that frown upon being questioned. Many of us experience an inner feeling that doesn't match with what we are being told or taught. Thus, I take this as a sign that we are reaching out to educate ourselves to an ever-expanding knowledge of our world and beyond.

I believe we choose to incarnate in this physical world to share our experiences with other souls before we are even born. Already having agreed to incarnate for learning experiences to aid our spiritual growth, that physical life has to offer. It may be impossible to learn or achieve all our spiritual lessons the first time around and we may have to come back again in another lifetime.

A mother will feel her unborn foetus move for the first time generally around 13 - 16 week of the pregnancy, referred to as the quickening. This I believe is the time when the soul first enters the biological suit of the foetus. The gender at this stage already determined. The soul can at will, enter and exit throughout the nine-month gestation.

I believe the soul to be present at the time of birth. As it is at the time of death. In almost all the spiritual readings I have given, there seems to be important to validate the manner of their passing. Often naming the hymns that were sung and of the variety of flowers that were present. This is an important time for the soul as it is the last day of their contract with their biological suit.

I wondered about the soul when one goes into a coma. Does it stay with your body or temporarily leave? Through my connection with my spirit team, I'd asked the question.

The way it has been described to me is that coma patients are not spiritually dead and the soul has not left the body. I describe it as a period of time where the soul is at rest, to make its karmic choice, whether to stay, or leave the body and go to the astral plane, a non-physical realm of existence.

I have been fortunate to have had many years' experience of working with brain injury and end of life clients and would like to share with you a compilation of the amazing ways they have found to communicate.

I am your Brother

I soon learnt as a medium that I can be utilised as an interpreter, for those not fully passed into spirit. To give validation to their loved ones here on the earth-plane from people who have suffered a traumatic brain injury and were not certified as being dead.

It was whilst giving a skype reading that I had described the image of the spirit communicator. He gave an account of the injury he had sustained after suffering a massive haemorrhage of the brain and fell down. He confirmed the gash to his forehead was made on impact to the side of the sink in his bathroom. He went on to confirm he was the sitter's brother.

The sitter had gone quiet on the other end of the phone, saying he was confused and had paused the session. He informed me his brother had not passed and was still alive.

Feeling rather confused I was assured by the spirit communicator he was his brother. In spirit communication, they may reveal brothers-in-law as brothers or mothers-in-law as mothers. I'd presumed this to be the case.

He went on to describe the sitter had a framed photograph of himself sitting on his bookshelf, wearing a red jumper. He paused for a moment more before replying he had such a picture.

The communicator in spirit revealed he was in fact, lying in a hospital bed on a neurological ward and was in a vegetative condition. I don't like to use the term vegetative, as it seems so final and harsh.

I must admit I was a little taken aback at his remark. I asked the sitter shall I continue? *"Yes, proceed and see what else transpires"* he'd said.

The sitter then asked the question of his brother, *"have you passed into the light, are you in Heaven"?* No, he said, *"I have one foot here in the earth plane and the other in the spirit world"*. He continued saying through me *"I cannot physically communicate to anyone because of the extensive damage to my brain, of which I am aware there is no cure"*. He went on to describe in detail of the communications he had heard from family members, who had visited him and had sat around his bedside. He said he was thankful for the Christmas presents he had received and validated what each one of them was.

He divulged the fact that he would choose the outcome when the time was right and had decided now, was not an appropriate time to fully enter the spirit realm as his daughter was studying hard and he did not want to disrupt her studies at this crucial time.

The sitter was not knowledgeable in the soul's journey and his experience in these matters was limited, however, he did gain an understanding on the process, once he was able to step back from his own emotion and see the bigger picture. He understood we are able to control to a certain extent our own journey.

Many people would have heard of the scenario that whilst sitting by your loved one's bedside, waiting for the final moment to occur, would need a visit the bathroom to come back to find they had passed.

Or when relatives have had to travel some distance in order to be beside them at the time to find they have been able to hold on those vital minutes prior to release.

Steven

In 1992 I was assigned to a young lad, Steven, who as a result of a motorbike accident had suffered a brain injury. He was placed in an induced coma, for some time, to allow the brain time to recover and the swelling to subside. He was clinically classified as being brain dead.

Steven was placed on a ventilator, a life support, as he was struggling to breathe unassisted. The prognosis was not favorable due to the extensive brain bleed. His family were told to prepare for the worst and after sufficient time, it was decided the ventilator was to be switched off.

Neurologists had tested every possible way of establishing if there were any nerve responses but results had shown there was far too much damage for the brain to recover. He was in a deep sleep and showing no signs of response. Basically, it was just a matter of time. His family wanted him home, close to them, where he would receive care, in a non-clinical environment.

His Mother had wanted to be the one to turn off the ventilator and whilst his parents together with his sister had stood around his bed, the breathing apparatus was removed. Although they were expecting the worse Steven took his first spluttered breath. He was now breathing unaided but would remain in a sleep state. His eyes were closed and it was not known for certain if he would be able to hear or not. There was no more the hospital could do for him and discharged him into the Agencies care.

His soul had decided to continue his journey here on the earth plane.

I was at his home awaiting his arrival by ambulance, his room had been adapted for his needs by his Father who was a builder.

It was after only a few months of working with him, daily that I started experiencing, what I thought were vivid dreams. Steven and I would meet and we talked at great lengths of his likes and dislikes and of his memories with his family. He showed himself to me as physically and mentally whole and able to move freely, with no limitations or disabilities. We discussed his preference for music and of his favourite band 'Iron Maiden' He told me of the posters that were once upon his bedroom walls but were now stored away in the attic.

The dream was so real it stayed with me the following day. I had formed a good relationship with Stevens's family and told his mother of my distinctive dreams, she stepped back with a look of shock on her face. She said, Iron Maiden was his favourite group, saying no more, she left the room.

When I arrived the following day, his walls were once more adorned with the posters of his favourite band. His mother had asked her husband to retrieve the posters and CD's from the attic.

The dreams became almost a nightly theme. In each dream, we talked at length of his medical condition and of his physical limitations. He was aware and without emotion saying he was fine, it is his choice to remain in this existing state. I asked about karma, he smiled and acknowledged this was his choice.

It came to mind that what I was experiencing could well have been astral travelling rather than lucid dreams. I had wondered if it was possible that we were communicating on another level in another astral dimension. I am often told by people of their dream experiences and their connection with their loved ones and that they could feel their hands upon their face, so real and yet so disappointing when awakening.

Many months had passed, when Steven awoke from his deep sleep. He opened his blue eyes that just stared ahead. Over time he gradually began to feel sensations of touch, sound, smell, and sight and had the ability to move one arm and one leg. We worked on how to communicate through blinking for yes and no responses. It was a wonderful breakthrough for him and his family especially considering his previous prognosis was poor.

I wanted to test our communication in daylight, through telepathy, during our waking times. The following day, whilst attending to him, I looked deep into his eyes and asked him through mental communication only, to give me a sign, anything that I could see or hear, to demonstrate to me he had the ability of telekinesis. He replied with a quick blink of yes. My co-worker had seen his response and asked what was he saying yes to, we hadn't asked him anything?

I'd noticed a slight movement in my peripheral view. A dream catcher, hanging in his window was moving very slightly. Standing there for some time I asked if he was responsible for the movement and could he move it faster. After a few moments, it did just that and began turning around and around at some speed. I heard a movement from outside his room and knew we were to be joined, looking up I noted it had stopped spinning. A few minutes had passed and all alone once again, I asked for validation. Within minutes it had started to spin around and stop directly when asking. I checked for any possible draughts to have caused this movement, there was none.
I believe Steven's mind can produce the energy to move objects. My co-worker was slightly freaked out by this and had felt very uncomfortable with it so I had stopped the communication with him.

What was interesting to note, is that over the years, the more communication we had received directly from Steven himself, the less frequent his astral visits were with me.

Over time Steven had regained some mobility and had become stronger. It was confirmed he could hear and see. Although he would never be the same as before the accident, his brain had recovered to a certain stage.

It's a Surprise

I reflected back to an incident I had experienced way back when I had worked for a private agency. I was assigned to looking after a lovely old gentleman, who resided in a private nursing home. He had mild dementia.

On entering his room one morning, he seemed rather anxious about having to pack his holdall with a few belongings. He informed me he was going on a trip. I enquired where he was going, he replied, it's a surprise but I do know its somewhere beautiful. I was bemused by this and kept up the banter.

He continued, saying his sister had told him last night when she had visited. He said she had talked of their parents being so excited by the reunion. I knew from his case notes; his sister had passed away some years previous and he did not have any visitors recorded in the book.

Never the less I continued to pack the items. His shoe cleaning kit, the daily newspaper, his razor set and his slippers and dressing gown were a few of the items suggested. I did as he had asked which seemed to have settled him.

I received a call from the agency early the following morning, informing me of his passing. He had died in his sleep. I knew in my heart, he was now re-joined with his family

The Silent Witness

It was December 2014 I was assigned to my new job working with a vulnerable adult. Carl lived independently with 24/7 care in his own specially adapted home which he had recently moved into. He had suffered a brain injury as a result of being a passenger in a road traffic accident (RTA) six years previously. He was unable to verbally communicate and had encountered many complex medical conditions. Sadly, his friend the driver had passed at the scene.

On my first shift and upon entering the property, I was warmly greeted by his mother, Diane, who showed me around identifying where the drugs cabinet was and where medical supply packs were stored. I became very dizzy and disorientated and even toppled slightly off-balance whilst standing beside his electronic bed, whilst going through the handheld controls. His mother had noticed this and asked if I was ok? Consciously I was listening to her but subconsciously I knew from experience; this was the effect of standing on a ley-line. The property was positioned straight opposite a church, of which are generally built upon crossing ley- lines or somethings as referred to Meridian earth lines.

One evening during my night shift and whilst sitting with his mother, strange phenomena started to happen. The room temperature had dropped dramatically. Diane held her arm up showing that her hairs were standing to attention. I'd grabbed my phone camera as from previous experiences of this nature, I knew something paranormal was about to happen and wanted to capture the moment.

Several seconds had passed, when a shaft of pure white light, cylindrical in shape, appeared. These tubes of light are thought to be portal openings, from where entry can be made from one dimension to another. Diane had also witnessed it. I was relieved as I had been able to capture it on my camera. The intense light had dispersed and in return, a mist had begun to gather. A beautiful lady was taking form. She wore a cornflower blue, two-piece suit and portrayed herself to me to be no more than 5ft in height with a slight build.

Clairvoyantly I'd asked who she was. She gave her name. Diane at this point could not see her but was aware of my distant glance. I gave the description along with the name of the woman when Diane immediately said that's my grandmother. That's the suit I choose for her to be buried in. I continued to relay her grandmother's message of which gave her a great deal of comfort. Her grandmother had also revealed a family secret and one Diane had not known about until this time. I cannot relay what that secret was as it was very personal to her family. She had later discussed what had been revealed to her mother when she had met up with her a few days later. Her mother had been shocked as she had already known of the secret and had validated the information was correct.

Diane had taken on a fascination of what she had just witnessed and wanted to understand more. I was happy in the knowledge that she now knew; I was a medium.

Over a period of three weeks or so, the electricity in the new purpose-built property seemed to have a life of its own. Taps and showers would turn on at all times during the day and night. This is a common paranormal occurrence and I have found from previous experience it is generally linked to deep-rooted emotions.

There had been several power cuts over a period of two days with no other property in the street experiencing the same thing. I met with the electrician who was called in to investigate the circuit board for any faults. He was totally baffled as none were found.

The occurrences were not just confined to Carls room, as a bedroom was provided for use by Co-workers who were on a sleeping night shift. On many occasions, the co-worker preferred to stay on the sofa in the lounge, due to the many strange experiences they had felt in the bedroom. Many had reported the bed quilt would be pulled off them and dragged down the bed followed by a heavy pressure felt, upon their chest, seeming to hold them down. Sparkly lights would appear and a dark shadowy figure had been seen standing at the foot of the bed. An overwhelming sensation of being watched was often felt.

Several weeks after he moved in, Carl suffered a medical setback and had to have an emergency operation. His health had deteriorated where he had encountered a chest infection. Surgery complications had caused him breathing difficulties and was placed on a breathing ventilator.

It was whilst sitting with Diane in the resuscitation unit, deep within the depths of a London hospital basement when I saw a spirit of a man. He was standing at the far end of the room and seemed to be focused on the papers he held in his hands. He had stood in front of a wall, of which was lined with a row of large oxygen cylinders.

His image was becoming clearer to me and I could see in more detail what he looked like. Diane was aware of my strange look and concentrated her gaze in the same direction. She asked, "*are you connected? Can you see something*"? Yes, I said and explained what I could see and feel. I'd described he was a stout gentleman with receding white hair and was a flamboyantly dressed individual. He wore a multicoloured tweed jacket and dickie-bow tie. I knew he was aware that I could see him and had turned briefly to look in my direction with a bemused expression on his face.

He had told me through mental mediumship that there had been an explosion, caused by these cylinders. His stance, changed as he stood back, and waved his arms towards them. However, he informed me this was not the cause of his passing but that it had been coincidental, as it had happened in the same time frame of his passing. I have found through experience that spirit finds time difficult to pinpoint and will generally indicate an event happening, around the same time frame.

Just then a fully gowned nurse had walked into the recuses unit and began checking the many monitor displays. Diane and I were the only people around which was a rare moment for a Saturday night.

Diane had asked her *"Do you know of a gentleman that wore a tweed jacket and dickie bow tie? He was short and had receding hair.* She pointed towards the end of the room and continued *"was there at any time cylinders on that wall"*? The nurse looked at her in surprise and acknowledged who the gentleman was. She told us he was a senior consultant and a much-respected surgeon. She confirmed the explosion of the cylinders and validated this was around the time of his passing, from a heart attack.

It was whilst I was engrossed in what the nurse was divulging about the consultant when I received a slight tap on my forearm. Upon turning around, I came face to face with the spirit of a young lady. Her age little difficult to distinguish as she had a well-worn face that could tell many a hardship and trauma. She looked in her late twenties, with blonde, shoulder-length hair. I caught a pleading gesture in her eyes as had looked at me. She slowly turned looking over her shoulder, her gaze fixated on the corridor behind her. Id felt she was beckoning me to look also. I saw a scene unfolding before me. Two gowned nurses were giving resuscitation working on either side of a hospital gurney. They were working desperately hard to save a life. I became aware of a movement, an arm had fallen free of the cover and had dangled down revealing puncture mark bruising, that ran down its entire length. The spirit of the young lady was now standing beside the trolley looking down at herself, observing the care that was being administered. She briefly glanced up at me, our eyes locked for seconds before she walked into a room further down the corridor. The nurses wheeled the gurney with the lifeless body of this young unknown woman, down the corridor and into a room. I was transfixed, speaking out loud of the images I was seeing giving a running commentary so that everyone present could hear.

Diane and the nurse simultaneously asked me to point out which door she had disappeared through. I had pointed out theatre room 2. There was a notice that read, 'Not in Use'. The nurse confirmed the theatre had been newly equipped with the latest operating gadgetry but was not currently in use due to electrical malfunctions. Numerous tests had been carried out but nothing had been found to have caused the faults and was deemed unfit for purpose.

The nurse was so fascinated by what had been said, she had paged another nurse on duty that night, working in another department to join her, when she could. Shortly we were joined by the other nurse. The incident of the young spirit woman was relayed to her. She had been one of the nurses administering resuscitation as shown in my image. She had not divulged the girl's name but did reveal she was a suicide victim who had for many years been struggling with a drug addiction.

The nurses had asked if I would go into theatre room 2 to check it out. They informed me the electrical faults had started not long after the woman had passed. *"Could there be a connection?"* they asked. Just then their bleepers sounded an alarm, an emergency had just come in requiring their attention. Unfortunately, we did not see either of them again and I was not given the opportunity to enter the disused operating room.

Once Carl was home from the hospital and during another shift, my co-worker and I were talking about the devastating loss of his mother who had died in his arms on Mother's Day two years previous. He was about to show me a picture of her then realising he must have left his mobile phone in his car, parked in the driveway, in front of the house. As he hadn't come straight back in, I stepped out of the door to use the key fob to close the electric gates. Glancing over, I could see his head bent down, looking behind and under his car seat, searching for his phone. Upon turning back towards the house, I noticed a large white box sitting on the doormat. I picked it up and brought it inside. He had come in a few minutes later with his phone in his hand. I told him I'd brought his box inside but he looked surprised saying it wasn't his. There was no labelling on the box but we opened the sealed lid. Inside were 6 iced cupcakes. 'Happy Mother's Day' was iced upon each one. Mother's Day had been the week prior.

Neither of us had seen this box before and it certainly wasn't on the doormat when we had opened the door. We'd felt each of the sponge cakes, they were stale. My co-worker asked, *"do you think this could this be a message from my Mother in spirit?"* It was certainly an apport, classified as a paranormal transference of an article appearing from an unknown source.

At that time, it was noted by all members of staff that Carl had started to display strange behaviour. His posture would change with an alert look on his face. His eyes would move as if following something invisible to us, often from one end of his large Open- plan room to the other. He'd then look up and smile, as if in recognition. A strange phenomenon would always occur shortly thereafter. Staff would often ask him if he was ok, he would reply by putting up his thumb, his yes response.

One of these phenomena included the shower in his wet room turning itself on for no apparent reason. 4.00 am seemed to be the most favoured time. Carl would often be asleep and oblivious to it happening. The TV in the lounge would change channels often selecting a sports channel. I'd asked him on several occasions if he was aware when something was about to happen, he smiled and seemed nonchalant but did answer yes.

Carl was an avid Man United football fan. Blu-tak had held in place miniature football figurines of his team. They were all lined up in a row and ran along the top of the large TV in the lounge. One by one they simultaneously began leaping off and landed in the centre of the room. It was fascinating to watch how energy can be manipulated but I did wonder why and to what purpose. Carl was not witness to this as he was asleep in bed at the time.

It was the eve of Carls Birthday; the house had been decorated with bunting that hung from the ceiling. Whilst he slept, the house had come alive. The bunting began to change from showing 'Happy Birthday' written upon each section to a picture of a spirit face, all depicting young males. Both I and my co-worker couldn't believe our own eyes. We sat amazed and watched these images appear all around us. We had managed to capture them on our cameras.

Then each of the pictures that hung on the wall began to change. Spirit faces would supersede the original image. The atmosphere had changed to an oppressive condition and I felt the energy was becoming dark. My co-worker was nervous and asked me to check out the staff bedroom. I found it was extremely active and I had felt there was more than one portal open. I had taken several pictures of the room where many spirit faces were captured, looking in, through the windows. We counted there were at least thirty different faces. As a result, my co-worker decided to sleep on the couch.

I placed a tape recorder in the room for a few minutes in the hope of capturing EVP. On rewinding it, we heard male voices but they were not clear enough to distinguish what was said. Loud bangs and a dragging sound were recorded but on entering the room nothing had been changed or altered.

Memories of my experience with Steven came to mind, I'd asked Carl if he was responsible for these things happening, he pointed his middle finger, his no response. "*Do you know who is then?*" I'd asked, he responded with thumbs up. He turned his head to end the conversation.

The other waking staff member had gone into Carls bedroom in the early hours to administer his medication via tube. He recalls walking into his room in stocking feet and upon entry into Carls room had experienced hearing footsteps like a woman's heels tip-tapping upon the wooden floor. When venturing further into his room, the footsteps faded, as if walking away.

It was in the early hours of the morning I had been sitting with Diane in the lounge. She had remained awake with me throughout my evening shift. I'd gone into the kitchen to make us coffee whilst Diane took photos around his bedroom whilst he slept. Id walked into Carl's bedroom with Diane's coffee in hand to witness seeing many spirits standing inside his see-through wardrobes. From their actions, I knew they were aware I could see them. We were amazed to note that Carl was transfiguring, his features were becoming someone else's. A young spirit girl had been captured on Diane's camera lying beside him. Her eyes were closed.

Diane was unnerved and had reached out for my arm. We went back into the lounge to have a closer look at the snaps she had taken. His bedroom was in clear view from where we were sat on the sofa, in the open -plan lounge. She had startled me when she jumped up and thrust the camera towards me. She looked very distressed saying "*his not there, his gone, take a look*". I zoomed into the clear image she had taken. The bedsheets were as flat as a pancake, there was no one there. However, a strange not fully formed human figure was sat at the end of his bed. She did begin to calm down after checking Carl was physically ok and fast asleep. I'd gone back into the lounge leaving Diane standing beside his bed looking down at him. I looked up when I heard her groan and could see she had jumped back, as if in shock.

She ran back into the lounge and grabbed her camera. She managed to take a picture of him whilst screaming "*it's not him, it's not him*". Lying in the bed was the driver of the car, his dead friend. The image was explicit showing the side of his face. Diane knew instantly it was him, as this was the last image she had seen of him when viewing him in the chapel of rest. His friend had blonde hair with a pale complexion whereas Carl was mixed race with dark hair and olive skin. I could see with my eyes, what the camera lens was picking up. Within no time at all Carl was back again in his bed. What a night it had been. I had felt frazzled and a little puzzled. I had no idea what was happening or why.

Diane was now calm but had a thousand questions to ask of me by way of trying to understand what had just happened. She continued to take more shots and the next photo image was even more bizarre. It had captured Carls Alsatian dog with his green neckerchief lying across his body. She confirmed this was his dog who had died some years previously.

She had asked me, "*could Carl allow his friend to take procession of his body, if so, where does Carl go*"? To that question, I had no answer.

The following day, Diane had asked Carl if he saw his friend and had named him, yes came his reply. She also asked him if he responsible for the things that happen around here, again he replied yes.

I wondered why his departed friend had not used my channels of communication and was asked by Diane if I could tap into his energy. It was whilst Carl was displaying his usual visual display of seeing and communicating with something walking around his room that I tapped in. Carl turned around and looked straight at me. Diane noticing this had asked him, "*can Gail talk with him*"? he looked at me a little longer before raising his thumb for yes.

Contact was made via mental mediumship with his departed friend. He had confirmed some memories of which Diane had validated, names of people and places were given. Through contact, I am able to sense the character vibration of the soul. I was sensing a character that liked his own way, a little too sure of himself and didn't like limitations placed upon him. I did feel there was a darkness with him, a troubled soul.

I'd asked Diane about the friendship between Carl and his friend. She mentioned they were very similar in nature and both on occasions had displayed a little aggression. She said, *"They were just normal loud hyperactive teenagers"*. However, their antics had often led them into trouble

One's characteristics are carried forward as we enter the spirit realm and it was evident that the pattern of poltergeist activity was more prominent when Carl was angry and destructive in his behaviour.
I had felt the poltergeist activity was brought about by the connection to Carl and his friend in spirit and were continuing to connect their energies, displaying assaults on those that would come in contact with him.

The negative activity, together with Carl's outbursts, had made it a turbulent workplace to be in. Staff were dropping off the package one by one. They were concerned for their safety due to the injuries they were sustaining. Carls mood swings and aggressive outbursts were making it a dangerous work environment. There was a need whilst giving care to be in close proximity to him where he would kick you in the face or head given the opportunity. He had kicked me under my chin and sent me flying across the room on several occasions whilst other staff members would get scratched and pinched.

An entity can attack our energy field if there is a weak spot or hole in our aura. Most of us have weak spots, made weaker by emotional stress. These entities are akin to astral parasites who actively interfere with our energies and emotions having an effect on atmospheres and places.

Diane was a clear example of this when she visited Carl one evening, after dropping off friends at a train station. Carl was asleep and had been in a good mood all day, a rare occurrence. The house was quiet with no activity, all was calm. As soon as she had entered the house, the atmosphere changed. Carl awoke in an aggressive mood, hitting out at everybody and began to pull on his medical tubes causing himself a physical injury.

The atmosphere within the home had dramatically changed from calm to one of tension. Diane's energy was chaotic and erratic. Her visit had upset the whole atmosphere.

She entered Carls room in an attempt to calm him. I along with my co-worker was sitting on the sofa in the lounge and witnessed a white flash of light surround Carls bedroom door and within that light, a female in a wheelchair was seen leaving Carls room. I'd grabbed my phone camera but was not quick enough to capture the image. I placed it in the recording mode and was rewarded with an EVP. We all heard the voice of an angry female screaming. Diane was frightened when hearing the voice and had deleted the recording immediately.

The following day another apport appeared. It was a photograph and was found lying on the floor. No one had identified it as belonging to them. It was a photo of Venice, showing people getting out of a gondola. By the look and style of their attire, I would say it was taken in the late fifties early sixties. I had placed it on the staff room notice board but after a week, no one claimed it as theirs. The landlord popped into the house for a routine maintenance check. He claimed the photo was his, it was his Mother in the picture when she was younger and prior to her disability. She had lived in the property prior to Carl moving in. She had had the house purposely built specifically for her disability as she was a wheelchair user. On looking closer, the female in the photograph was the same lady we had seen in the white light coming out of Carls room. The landlord informed us Carls bedroom was once her own and that was where she had died. He remarked she wasn't a nice lady and could be very cantankerous.

Summary:
An entity will find someone suitable, often with similar emotional characteristics to themselves. They will try to invade the host's energy field, thereby depleting the host's life force and impose their own emotions upon them. Carls personality was very similar to his friends.

Diane had become a target herself as her emotional stress increased her inability to control her mood swings and she became intolerable to be around. Carls energy together with her own began to work against each other. It is known that a person's negative energy can and does create a knock-on effect on the atmosphere within the environment.

I believe several portal openings had been created. These portals, or invisible doors, allow passage from our existence to another dimension, often enticing for a low entity gate crasher to enter.

The staff began to disengage from this package, no longer happy to be physically attacked by Carl, or verbally by his mother. His continued independent living at home had come to an end, due to the lack of staff support.

He resides now in a neurological centre where he has the medical help he needs and where there are restrictions on visitors.

Chapter 10

IT

To date, this is one of the most disturbing cases of poltergeist activity I have ever been involved in. Its total focus seemed to be concentrated on a 14-year-old boy. I will refer to him by his pseudonym Jay.

Irene was the matriarch of the family. She asked for my help with her grandson, Jay. During our conversation, she gave a brief account of the activity of what her family have been experiencing over the last two years. Irene told me she felt like a prisoner in her own home and that other family members were not allowed to go out of the house at the same time. She remarked, *'IT doesn't like it.'*

'It' was the name of the entity given by the family. I could hear the desperate tone of her voice. She was at the end of her tether saying, *'Alan's not well and could really do without the stress.'* Alan is her husband, Jay's grandfather. It was hard to comprehend the extent of destruction she had mentioned they were experiencing.

I'd asked if she was happy for me to visit her at her home and to meet with Jay. She preferred our first meet to be just between us and away from the house. She suggested her friend's house for the meeting. It was only a few doors away from her own. Irene gave consent for me to record the session.

I'd learnt that Jay had gone to live with his maternal grandparents two years previous. Their daughter, Jay's mother, was under threat by the council to lose her home if things did not improve. Jay, as a juvenile, was also under scrutiny. He was attracting attention from the many things that were happening whilst at school.

Irene said, '*It was a few days before Christmas. It had been a dull day with periods of persistent rain. Jay and his mum were sat in the lounge watching a programme on tv when a large rock hurtled through the window shattering the glass. It landed in the centre of the floor. My daughter picked up the rock and then dropped it immediately. The rock was extremely hot and had burnt her hand. They immediately looked to see if they could see anyone outside. Even with a great view of the street from their home, they could see no one.*' Their house position gave them a clear view of the road ahead. Alan had gone around later that night and placed a wooden board to secure the home until the council could come and replace the window.

Within days of this incident, they started experiencing loud knocks and hammering bangs on the front door, at varying times, throughout the night. This was beginning to be a regular occurrence. *Irene noted, 'It was so loud it awoke their neighbours. They even started banging on their adjoining wall.'* Their relationship, with their neighbours, had begun to break down.

'Jay's mood swings became volatile over the coming weeks.' Irene stated. *'His mum felt she was walking on eggshells around him. He would flare up verbally over the smallest of things.'* She had received a letter from his school informing her of a string of incidents, they felt Jay was responsible for. She was asked to attend a meeting with the headmaster to discuss his behaviour. His teachers had become concerned about his demeanour. He seemed thinner and paler and was non-communicative with teachers and his peers. Irene shook

her head softly when she said, *'His personality deteriorated further over the coming weeks. It was felt in his best interest that a welfare officer was to be appointed to him.'*

A female welfare officer had come to Jay's home to gain an insight into his daily life. The home was clean with tired sparse furnishings. She was concerned by the amount of damage in the house. The walls, doors and most of the windows were damaged. The windows held no glazing and had been boarded up. She left to write up her assessment of the situation. A few minutes had passed when she returned. She said she must have left her phone as it was not in her bag. When they looked around, they found the phone lying on the tv unit. But that wasn't the only thing missing.

When the welfare worker went to fill her car with petrol later that evening, she found all her money had disappeared from her purse. Her credit cards hadn't been touched. Around sixty pounds of notes and some odd bits of change had all but vanished. Her bag had been beside her throughout the meeting.

Jay's mother was heading for a breakdown as her coping strategies were poor. She confronted Jay, *'What is happening with you. If you don't stop, you'll be taken into care.'* He'd snapped and started yelling, *'You're just like the rest of them, always finding fault with me and accusing me all the time.'* He ran out of the room slamming the door behind him. Minutes later, big loud banging noises came from upstairs. His mother went to investigate. Whilst walking up the stairs, she saw Jay standing on the landing with a transfixed look on his face. He said nothing. He just watched her as she had approached him. She told me she had felt very unsettled being around him as he was so unpredictable. His face had been as white as a sheet. She had noticed all the doors had been slammed shut making the landing appear dark. Suddenly, a loud thudding noise came from beside her making her jump. She was witnessing fist shaped puncture holes materialise. Without any apparent cause, each of the doors, one by one were being damaged. When she told the story to Irene, she said, *'Jay wasn't anywhere near doors at the time. He can't be held responsible.'* This had really scared Jay's mum.

Jay had a frown on his face as he looked at the damaged doors. Glancing back to his mum, he asked, *'what have you done?'* She was shocked. She couldn't say anything. He turned and walked slowly into his room, closing his damaged door quietly behind him. Irene said in a quiet voice, *'She had admitted to me of being a little frightened of her own son.'*

Whilst walking back down the stairs, the tv had turned itself on in the lounge. The volume on full was blaring throughout the house. She ran into the room where she could see the volume image displayed on the tv. The volume was at its maximum level. She frantically searched for the remote to the tv. Then, the radio, placed on the sideboard, had also turned itself on. A dull thudding sound was heard coming from an unknown source. The volume was raised higher and higher, whilst the radio fluctuated between channels. She couldn't locate the remote, so she pulled the plugs out of the socket to the tv and took the batteries out of the radio. Something had caught her attention in her peripheral view. She saw the tv was physically floating in the air for a mere few seconds. Without warning, it came down with a crash. The dull thudding had been someone frantically banging on her front door. Jay had remained upstairs throughout.

Still shaken by all that happened, she opened the door. Two police officers and her angry neighbour stood together. They had informed her they had received a complaint. The officers asked about Jay and if they could have a word with him. She called out Jay's name from the bottom step of the staircase. *'Is he okay?'* they had asked. Irene was amused and said, *'The neighbour raised his voice accusing my daughter of hitting her son. He confirmed they could hear the sounds coming through the thin walls all the time.'* The officers' expression was of concern.

Jay's mother became extremely agitated by their questioning. She asked the officers why they were wanting to see him. She was walking them through to the kitchen when the doorbell started ringing. It had a continual buzzing sound reverberating throughout the house. Jay's mother went to the front door. No one was there. One of the police officers had followed her believing it could have been the angry neighbour returning. She told the officer while shaking her head, *'the bell doesn't work.'* The officer chased traced the doorbell wire with his eyes. He saw that is was no longer connected to its junction. He even pressed the doorbell out of curiosity, but it didn't make a sound. She again called out to Jay for him to come downstairs saying the police were here and wanted a word with him.

The officers asked if they could just take a quick look around. On entering the lounge, they saw the tv in bits. There were parts scattered all over the floor. They asked if anyone else was in the house, enquiring about Jay's father. She informed them that he was not part of their life. He left when Jay was just a baby. Looking at the tv, Jay's mum tried to explain there had been an accident. The other officer started to go upstairs as Jay had not come down. He had noted the puncture compressions to each door asking, *'Who has the temper?'* he asked. Jay came out of his room and stood face to face with the officer. Irene said, *'luckily, nothing else took place, but my daughter was very shaken by the entire ordeal.'*

The following day, another large stone had been thrown through the dining room window, shattering it. Jay's mother remarked the rock was the same shape and size as before. The rock was hot to touch just as the previous one was. They had looked outside but no one was seen. They looked to see if there were any similar around the place. They couldn't find any. Later that day, a further two stones had been thrown through kitchen windows. Both of these windows were located at the rear aspect of the house within an enclosed garden.

The council had agreed to repair the damage but had placed a report as to the damage being suspect. Irene stated, *'They reprimanded my daughter. They said she would be billed for any further repair works as it was becoming a regular occurrence. Then they suggested that she reports the incident to the police.'*

Mother and son were no longer talking. They tried to avoid each other as much as possible. He had lost interest in anything she had suggested and preferred to stay alone in his room. His friends no longer came over to the house. She did attempt to strike up a conversation with Jay when they had bumped into each other outside the bathroom. She told he needs to spend some time outside of the house as he was becoming a recluse. He was not attending school which was sure to raise concerns. Irene, feeling the defeat of her daughter said, *'She felt she didn't have any parental control over him.'* He raised his voice to her and became very angry. Unexpectedly, and with great force, her bedroom door started swinging open and slamming shut. This carried on for several minutes.

She tried to stop it from shutting, but the force was so strong it knocked her off balance. *'Make it stop Jay, she screamed, make it stop.'* Almost immediately it did. He turned his back on her and walked back into his room saying out loud, *'IT doesn't like you!'*

A social worker arrived later that week to carry out an assessment of Jay's mother for psychological distress. Irene said, *'They were beginning to think my daughter was not coping and was unfit to look after her son. Jay was examined by his GP. There were no physical signs of abuse or neglect noted.'*

He was barely attending school. Every time he did attend, an incident would happen where he would always be blamed for orchestrating it. On one occasion, whilst Jay was in his chemistry class, his Bunsen burner was witnessed flying off from his workspace and narrowly missed hitting a fellow pupil. Other times, wherever Jay sat, light bulbs would explode just above his head and often as Jay had walked past a row of books, in the library, they flew off their shelves. They scattered in different directions. Not a day went by without some form of activity. Pupils were becoming unnerved in his presence. It was decided, that the Headmaster would bear the sole responsibility for teaching him in all his subjects.

Jay's grandparents had paid to replace all the upstairs doors. They feared for their daughter's well-being and suggested Jay spend the weekends at their home to give their daughter a break. Jay loved his weekend visits as he was close to his Grandparents. His Grandfather had bought him an Air fix model of an army tank for them to work on together. The box contained glue, an instruction manual and four pots of paint in a range of army colours. Jay was keen to start making the model. He was looking forward to working on it when he got home from school later that day. At school that day, his paranormal activity had been horrendous. Jay had been accused of being responsible for everything that had happened. Teachers had taken to giving him a wide berth when passing him in the corridors. They were worried in case they got caught up in any incident. The head master was in his office giving Jay his history lesson when the head master's papers flew off his desk and onto the ground. Every time he tried to retrieve them, the papers would move away out of his reach. The head lost his temper and told Jay, *'I am not amused by your silly pranks. You can leave this room now!'* Jay was fuming. To think yet again he had been held responsible for something that wasn't his fault. On the other hand, he was somewhat amused to have seen the Head crawl around on his hands and knees.

Jay was stood outside, in the corridor. He heard the screeching voice of alarm from the head master. When he opened the door, the Head was standing there with an array of army coloured paints dripping all over his head and shirt. Behind him, lined up on his desk, were 4 small tins of army Air fix paint. All their lids were missing. The head master screamed, *'Get out, get out.'* Once Jay was home at his grandparents' house, he noticed the Air fix box was still perfectly sealed. He opened the box and saw there wasn't any paint within its contents. His grandfather's home was some seven miles from the school. That was Jay's last attendance at school. A social worker had been appointed to Jay. Once a week, she would bring a schedule of school work by for Jay to complete. Irene informed me, that nothing strange had happened when Jay had been visiting them.

Christmas day had arrived. Jay and his mum spent the day with his grandparents. Whilst sitting around the table having lunch, Jay shared a Christmas cracker with his grandmother. The prize flew out of the cracker, in Jay's direction. It was an oversized dice. As Jay went to retrieve it, it had jumped away from his grasp just as the papers had done when the headmaster had reached out. His family were all witness to this. Every time Jay went to pick up the dice, it would move away from him, so he couldn't grasp it. This happened on every occasion. Time and time again, as he placed his hand near the dice, it flipped over. His grandfather had asked Jay to think of a number. Jay said, '*Number four*' and the dice flipped over to reveal the number four. Jay then called out, '*Number six*' and it flipped to number six. This went on. With each number he asked, the dice rolled that number. Everyone else had a go to make the dice move, but it never did. They were all bemused by the dice as they couldn't figure out how it was done.

It was agreed, with Jay's blessing, he would temporarily move-in with his grandparent's full time. This was much to his mother's relief. Unfortunately, it wasn't long before sharp knives, scissors and kitchen implements began to disappear from their usual places. One evening, whilst they were all sitting around the dining room table, they had seen a bread knife materialise. It was suspended in mid-air, right in front of them. After a few seconds, it dropped. Seconds later they heard a clicking sound, the wall cupboards began to open. Cupboard by cupboard with the crockery flying out in every direction.

Jay's mother ran out of the room screaming while dodging the flying plates. She screamed, '*Bad things only happen when you're about Jay!*' He vehemently reacted to her outburst and denied being responsible.

The kitchen seemed to take on a life force of its own. Drawers opened and then slammed shut. The lights were flashing on and off. The toaster, coffee maker and canisters, all went crashing to the floor as if an invisible hand had swiped the worktops till the countertop was free of all the accessories. Irene noted, '*Jay did not seem to be disturbed by the incident.*' This was the first time his grandparents had actually been witness to the phenomena.

157

His grandfather spoke up saying, *'Leave the boy alone! He hasn't left his seat. He can't be held responsible.'*

We were what I would expect to be halfway through our meeting. Irene was in mid-sentence when she had received a phone call on her mobile. After she answered the phone, she sighed, *'Oh no.'* I could see she was physically shaken. Her eyes were wide, darting around the room, as she was listening. She was still digesting the information when she stood up gathering her things. She apologised for having to cut the meeting short, but she had to go. She had told me, *'The call was from Jay. The vacuum cleaner had turned itself on. The vacuum hose was thrashing around the room, narrowly missing his elderly grandfather.'*

I asked, *'Can I accompany you back to your home?'* Unfortunately, she was reluctant for me to go with her. She wanted time to discuss my possible visit with the family first. I did not press her further but had hoped it would be soon. We left the neighbours home together. I sat in my car and watched Irene walk the few steps down the path towards her own home. It was evident to see which house was hers. All the windows had been boarded up.

A few days later, I received a phone call from Irene. Her voice was very weary. She said she was tired of it all and that I was her last hope. She revealed to me, that over the months, several paranormal groups had conducted experiments. All of which were fruitless. The only paranormal thing they experienced whilst being here was that they had all lost their money. Their wallets and purses were emptied. We now tell everyone who comes into this house, please leave your bags and keys in your car. A vicar was also appointed to bless the home but that didn't work either.

They had salvaged as much furniture as possible. They put as much as they could in the garden shed. The bigger items of furniture were being stored at her daughter's house, as no further incidents had taken place since Jay had moved out. Irene had appointed me to take the case.

I had asked the family to meet with me in a public location away from the home. They were nervous but had agreed. Irene wanted Alan to remain at home due to his illness. She would be accompanied by Jay and his mother. Irene chose a coffee shop within a large department store, in their local town.

This was their first outing as a family in two years. Irene explained they were frightened of the consequences of their actions, but everything else they tried had failed. On meeting Jay for the first time, he did not speak. He only nodded in acknowledgement. He had worn a cap, with the peak slightly concealing his dark eyes. His eyes held no emotion. It was difficult to read his features which made me feel slightly uneasy. Like Jay, I made sure my expression was giving nothing away. I'd asked him if he was frightened of IT? His monosyllabic reply was, *'No.'* Irene shot a quick nervous look towards her daughter. Both had kept their heads bent low. You could see the tension in their bodies. I asked Jay, *'Does IT talk to you?'* Jay replied, *'Yes.'*

I had learnt from Irene of the strange phenomena they had been experiencing since Jay had come to live with them. She told me that news soon got around the estate of the strange things that were happening. Jay's mum mentioned, *'Often when I had visited Jay at my mother's home, I would notice a small group of people taking photographs of the house with its boarded-up windows. On one occasion a local reporter had come to visit the property to take photographs and had written an account of the events. Mum allowed this to happen in the hope that we would find the right help to resolve our torment.'*

She continued to tell me of the bizarre phenomena experienced by Jay's visiting social worker. *'During her one to one with Jay, she was sitting in the lounge. Out of nowhere, she started feeling heavy droplets of water landing on her head. It was raining indoors. The water was appearing out of mid-air. Outside, it was a warm and sunny day. She got to her feet and moved. She thought she could get away from the leak. Instead, it had moved with her and kept following her wherever she went. Nowhere else in the lounge was wet.'* Fast flowing water was beginning to run down the bannister rail in the hallway. On examination, there was no cause for it. It did not seem to have a source. *'She had taken photos and even a video, as she knew others would not believe her. She had collected a sample in a small container of which was later analysed as being rainwater.'*

'The social worker had stepped outside looking to leave the property.' Jay's mum continued, *'She was talking with my mum on the doorstep when she experienced a thud on the top of her head. She looked up, thinking something had fallen from the window above. When she looked down, she saw a fifty pence coin beside her feet. Seconds later another coin had fallen. Within minutes it was raining money. £5.00 and £10.00 bank notes were wafting down through the air. Coins, of every denomination, were dropping right in front of her. It was all contained in a small region of the front garden. Some neighbours witnessed what was happening. They ran got saucepans and bowls to collect the falling money. Even the postman got in on the action. He received his bonus that day. He just held his bag open and collected whatever was falling. My mum had held out her apron to collect what she could. The social worker was stunned and rooted to the spot as she saw a menagerie of excited people running around her with a variety of receptacles. It had disturbed her to such a degree that she refused to visit again.'*

I noted that Jay was giving the impression of being disinterested. He had not interacted with the conversation in the slightest. Neither did he participate with any of the comments or remarks made throughout the meeting. I thought now was a good time to depart the café and head back to Irene's house. I wanted to see if anything would happen on entering the property, especially as they had gone out as a family, against IT's wishes.

Irene told me they had travelled by bus. I offered to drive them home, as it was only a short journey in my car. Jay seemed keen. Irene needed convincing. She said, *'The last time all of us travelled in a car together, sharp implements appeared and were thrown around inside. Scissors, knives even garden shears had appeared.'* On enquiring who had been hurt, she replied, *'No one.'* I decided to take the risk.

I had parked in the car park underground and whilst placing my ticket in the machine to pay the fee, the digital display kept fluctuating between £1.50 and 8888. I was reluctant to offer my ticket with the possibility of it getting stuck. It was evident that when Jay stood in front of the machine, the display read 8888. Irene also noticed the strange display. When she pulled Jay back towards her, it displayed £1.50. I didn't mention it at this stage, but I did wonder if this was being influenced by Jay's electromagnetic field. I thought back to the Dice incident and of the way it had reacted when Jay had placed his hand near it, acting as a form of telekinetic energy.

Jay had sat directly behind me in the back seat his mother was beside him. I could feel his eyes upon me reflected in the rear-view mirror. There weren't any incidents on the journey.

Once we arrive at their home, I deliberately left my handbag in the car. I only took my camera with me. Irene was the first to enter her home. She quickly walked through to the lounge to check if everything was ok. I could see her body tense as she walked through the threshold. Alan announced nothing had happened whilst they had been out.

As I entered their home, I was shocked. I couldn't believe what I was seeing as my eyes took in a 360-degree view around the room. The property looked like a war zone. What resembled bullet holes, were seen on every wall. The house was bare of plants, flowers, pictures and ornaments. The atmosphere was cold and uninviting. Lino flooring ran throughout the house. The open fireplace had been shut off with various types of wood. All the windows had been boarded. Irene looked embarrassed, bless her. She had noticed my stare towards the fireplace. Irene said, *'It was necessary to board up the fireplace due to large volumes of human excrement that would come down the chimney.'* I had no words.

The black leather couch, minus any legs, were pushed against the wall. They were at the far end of the open lounge. It bore splits and tears. *'How did these happen?'* I asked pointing to the damage. She replied, *'IT does it when he gets angry.'* Irene could see my eyes focus on a large hole in the wall. She said, *'That's where the BT phone socket used to be. IT doesn't like us to have a phone. We've had eight phone sockets installed over a short period of time. No sooner has the BT van driven off, when IT pulls it out. The socket, together with most of the wall.'*

I took a seat on the sofa. I was placing my polystyrene cup of coffee on the floor when I noticed an object come flying through the air. It was heading straight for me. On instinct, I moved sideways. The object had come in contact with the boarded window behind me and had landed on the window seal. I grabbed the object, but I had to drop it instantly as it was extremely hot. I grabbed it again a few seconds later, worried it may disappear. It was a half-opened packet of polo mints. The foil wrapping was acting as a conductor to heat. I'd unwrapped the paper and had poured the contents out to find the dense mints had become like talcum powder in texture. I thought it very strange that not one of the family members rushed over to investigate.

I sat back down on the sofa. Something fell in front of me, landing in my lap. It had made me jump as I was concerned it may have been a sharp object. It was only a bar of chocolate minus the wrapping. In the top right-hand corner was an indentation of m's and w's the sign of a small child's bite mark. Jay was sat opposite me and had looked bemused. I asked the question of him, *'Is IT responsible for this Jay?'* He replied, 'Yes.'

I offered Jay the chocolate bar as a joke. I wanted to get a reaction out of him. The other family members had laughed. Jay was not amused. His half-full bottle of Vimto, that stood on the floor in front of him, took off at great speed, like a rocket. It had caused an impression on the ceiling when it struck. When it fell back to the ground, it did so in slow and controlled motion. Irene screamed, *'Oh no!'* while placing her hands upon her head. She cried, *'IT's really angry now!'* *'Wow.'* I commented, *'That was good, can he do that again?'* Jay's face held a look of annoyance.

My attention was drawn back towards the rips and tears on the sofa. Irene had told me, *'These were caused by sharp flying objects. Can you believe, this sofa is only three years old? It was a beautiful suite with matching armchairs.'* She continued saying, *'One evening, we were all in the lounge. Jay was sitting in the armchair when it started to vibrate and move from side to side'.* Alan found his voice and had confirmed the chair had spun around at speed making Jay feel sick. *'It had frightened him*

Irene interjected. We did try holding onto the chair, but it sent us both flying to the floor'.

I received a message from a tv personality whose speciality lies as a paranormal researcher and author. She had featured on a tv series highlighting accounts of hauntings during the mid-nineties. Somehow, she had heard about this case and had contacted me through a social media site, wanting to meet with me. Against, my better judgement, I'd thought having a demonologist on board would be advantageous. I reluctantly introduced her and her boyfriend to Irene's family. Irene took the couple around the house, giving them a running explanation as to how the damage had been caused. She even mentioned how on some occasions, when opening the oven door, hundreds of used and dried tea bags would fly out. They no longer use the oven. They have resulted in using plastic knives and forks and polystyrene cups and plates.

I'd caught the look of excitement from the personality towards her boyfriend. I had felt very uneasy and wished I had never agreed to meet with them. Every time I had suggested something, she would dismiss it, taking over. Her boyfriend suggested that he retrieves his cameras from the car. We were all stood in the hallway, near the front door, waiting for him. The telephone table started levitating some inches off the ground. It then began to fly through the air at mid-height. Irene went into her protective posture, clutching her head and shielding herself from any flying debris. The personality was terrified. She ran out of the house and onto the front lawn. I took off after the table. It was manoeuvring itself through the doorways with precision. It ended its journey by falling out of the air in front of the back door.

This experience had clearly unnerved the personality but also got her excited. I overheard a call she had made on her mobile to her agent. She was talking about this case how the house had been destroyed and that it was the best paranormal activity she had seen. I could see from her reaction she did not get what she had wanted.

I began to have a different idea about this case. The parking machine incident kept going over and over in my mind. There was no doubt that paranormal events were taking place. The focus was definitely on Jay, but I felt there was something that I had overlooked. Some factors weren't adding up. The incident with the Christmas cracker, along with the parking machine, had shown me that Jay was demonstrating a form of telekinetic energy. It reminded me somewhat of a case I had heard of way back in the eighties with Matthew Manning. I had seen Matthew demonstrate his ability when I attended a show and saw him on stage perform a healing to which blew me away. I have always admired Matthews work and his amazing ability to heal. He had also experienced poltergeist type activity such as Jay, but he was found to have an extraordinary gift of being able to heal and turn unhealthy human cells into healthy cells just by his thought and the touch of his hands.

I had felt, with the right guidance, that Jay may be able to control the energy produced and steer it into a worthwhile cause. From previous experiences of this nature, I knew this was not merely a haunting. There was much more to it. The energy output did seem to have a connection controlled by Jay's mood. I wanted to put my theory to the test. I needed to try something to see if I was in the right thought process.

I needed to goad Jay into getting a response. I told him, *'I don't feel there is enough here. The site hasn't been very active. Other than the levitating table, there hasn't been any action. All the damage to the home was from previous assaults. I've not actually witnessed anything for myself apart from a packet of polo mints being thrown at me and a half-eaten chocolate bar landing in my lap.'* I stood up, laughing, with a pretence to leave.

The personality was happy as she wanted me out of the way, that I later found out was, for other honourable reasons. Jay's expression told me he wasn't happy. As soon as I had stood up to go, the lounge door had slammed shut. Irene's cigarettes and lighter had flown across the room hitting the back of the door. I took notice of Jay's body language and it was tense. He stood up and began pacing while rubbing his hands together. He was agitated, like a boxer prior to a match. This was showing me he had a conscious control over his actions and that this was not an entity at work.

I told Irene about Matthew Manning. We spoke of some of his experiences as a child and that I thought there was a similarity between him and Jay. I asked for her permission to talk to the research for physical phenomena in Cambridge. They were interested and agreed to meet with Jay and his grandmother. This was beyond Irene's life experiences. She had never travelled, and her circle of friends was small. She struggled. It was hard for her to comprehend all that I was trying to explain. Even though I tried to break it down, it was just too much for her.

The tv personality had overheard my conversation. She had her own theory. This didn't help Irene's already confused state of mind. I knew the personality (her name won't be revealed) wanted to take over the case in the hope of highlighting it as a potential tv series. I was deeply disappointed in her character. These people needed help, not a tv show. The fact she ran out of the room because of a levitating table also cast doubt on what help she could actually offer or even if she was a demonologist. She showed no interest in Jay displaying psychokinesis or telekinesis ability or of him having an influence over the control of energy being displayed. Jay was in a very vulnerable position of being utilised and miss managed. He was looking for answers himself and was keen to meet with the professors in Cambridge.

I'd received a call from Irene the following day, just prior to leaving my home to meet with them. She had informed me that she had thought hard about my proposal of taking Jay for tests to Cambridge and was not happy to go ahead. She was apologetic and sounded very stressed that I could not insist any further. She was mumbling the fact that she didn't want Jay as a lab rat undergoing probes and testing. She kept repeating that he was not mad, just disturbed. I added it was a shame as I'd felt we may have got some answers. I assured Ivy, *'I'm here as you invited me to help. To help Jay, I need to look at every possibility as to the cause of such phenomena, especially as I know it is very different from the normal type of poltergeist activity I see.'*

Irene had politely asked me to stand down as she couldn't deal with the stress involved. I did feel empathy for her and her family. She had been frightened off. My last words to her regarding Jay were, *'Please don't sign any documents without getting a solicitor to look at them first.'* She had agreed to do that.

I did feel the strong impression that the tv personality was standing beside her at the time of her call and that she had spoken of fabricated tests that I had wanted Jay to undergo. She and her boyfriend had stayed the night with Irene and the family.

I felt I had let Jay down, and there was nothing I could do. Irene had my telephone number should she wish to call me. A few nights later, my son who was staying with me and who was a computer enthusiast, woke me up around 3 am. He had asked me to look on my social media page as someone was slating me.

That, someone, was the tv personality. There were a further seventeen personas all giving comments under her own. All seventeen personas bore no facial images, just their names. The comments were derogatory to me and my work as a medium. My son had looked into the addresses and had informed me they were all from the same IP account and by the same person, her. Why did she feel the need to do such a thing? It shocked me. She had already convinced Irene I was sending Jay to the mental institute. I was no longer associated with the case.

I telephoned the fraud department of the social media site in America and had explained the situation. A screenshot of the comments had been taken and sent over to the fraud department. They had confirmed what my son had said. They were all composed of the same IP address, the same one as the tv personality. They had informed her that I had made the complaint and that they had the proof that she was responsible. I was asked if I wanted to sue her for defamation of character but remembering her loose tongue and of the fact she owed a lot of people money, what was the point. The media site had banned her from her inappropriate action. I had no further dealings with her.

Many months later, I received a message from Jay himself. He had contacted me on a social media chat box. He wanted my help. It was information on how to sue the tv personality. Id asked what had happened. Jay had felt badly let down and violated. The tv personality had placed cameras all around the home and had filmed a reality type show. She had also shown recorded interviews with Jay and his family members; placing them on YouTube. I told him she had acted illegally and that he was an underage juvenile. He had informed me that his grandmother had

168

given consent to the filming as his guardian by signing papers. I was so angry at Irene for being so gullible. He told me he had spoken to the tv personality and told her to take them off YouTube, she had declined.

Jay informed me she could no longer film as IT had destroyed all her electrical items along with expensive professional cameras. Sadly, relations between him and his grandmother had been strained.

I never went back!

26863043R00094

Printed in Great Britain
by Amazon